THE
AXIOMS
OF
Religion

THE
AXIOMS
OF
Religion

REVISED EDITION

Herschel H. Hobbs
and
E. Y. Mullins

BROADMAN PRESS
Nashville, Tennessee

© Copyright 1978 ● Broadman Press.

All rights reserved.

4217-07

ISBN: 0-8054-1707-9

Dewey Decimal Classification: 230.6

Subject Headings: BAPTISTS//BAPTISTS—DOCTRINES

Library of Congress Card Catalog Number: 78-50799

Printed in the United States of America

Dedicated to

EDGAR YOUNG MULLINS

whom I never knew personally
but who through his books has
been my teacher through the years

Contents

Introduction 9

1. "Who Are These Baptists, Anyway?" 13

2. Baptists and Denominationalism 25

3. The Historical Significance of Baptists............41

4. The Theological Axiom
   The Holy and Righteous God Has the Right
   to Be Sovereign 56

5. The Religious Axiom
   All Men Have an Equal Right to Direct Access
   to God 75

6. The Ecclesiastical Axiom
   All Believers Have a Right to Equal Privileges
   in the Church 91

7. The Moral Axiom
   To Be Responsible the Soul Must Be Free 111

8. The Religio-Civic Axiom
   A Free Church in a Free State 128

9. The Social Axiom
   Love Your Neighbor as Yourself 145

10. Facing the Future 161

Introduction

We are living in an era characterized by critical analysis. No one or nothing is regarded as immune to its probing examination. Heroes both past and present are called to stand before its judgment. Institutions long taken for granted are laid bare before its peering gaze as if they must justify their existence. The Bible itself is placed under the microscope of reason and in the test tubes of criticism.

In such an atmosphere religion itself has not escaped critical examination. Its basic tenets of faith are summoned to justify their right to be accepted. This is true even in the Christian family. In what hitherto has been regarded as the closed system of Roman Catholicism, some of its leading scholars are raising questions regarding many of its traditionally accepted beliefs. At the same time strong conservatives among Roman Catholics resist any liberal trends in that body. One of the more evident examples of this is the use of native languages instead of Latin in their rituals. Catholic laymen are demanding a larger role in the affairs of their church. The Roman Catholic Church is no longer the monolithic structure it was once regarded to be.

The element of change is even more prevalent in the atmosphere of the greater freedom of thought in other areas of Christendom. For more than a hundred years traditional theology and the nature of the Scriptures have been under attack. For more than a generation many religious bodies have become oriented more toward a social approach to the gospel than toward the personal and spiritual elements of evangelism. A television documentary "Born Again" presented the latter as if it were confined to certain groups and/or geographical areas of the nation. (It is of interest to note that in reply to a question as to the meaning of "born again," "Dear Abby," a Jewess, said that it means a personal faith in Jesus Christ.)

Evangelism is presented as if it were the exception rather than the norm in evangelical Christianity. One often wonders if, should the founders of certain branches of Christianity return, they would recognize the work they started.

For more than a generation denominationalism has been under attack by the ecumenical movement. It has been regarded by many as an evil, the scandal of the body of Christ as an obstacle in the path of Christian ministry to a complex world. Today ecumenicalism is under attack and/or its effectiveness questioned even among its friends, as they consider whether such is feasible or even desirable. In recent years the National Council of Churches has come into question, especially among the laity of its cooperating bodies, because of its authoritative(?) pronouncements in the fields of politics and economics. This has been largely due to small groups within the body claiming to speak for so many millions of Christians, the reported numbers within the cooperating denominations.

However, this critical examination of Christianity has not been without its blessings. It has led conscientious people on a search for the basics in the Christian faith. For instance, a few years ago in Great Britain a scholarly study commission raised serious questions regarding infant baptism. World upheaval has demanded a restudy of the purely social approach to the needs of humanity. A current study is being made across denominational lines as to the future of evangelicalism in America. Serious students of the Christian faith have been asking one vital question. When all the outward trappings have been removed from Christian bodies, what is it that remains which comprises the New Testament message that our world needs and wants to hear?

The purpose of this volume is an attempt to answer this question. What are *the axioms of religion* that form this bedrock message? An *axiom* is a self-evident truth which when seen needs no proof of its reality. The contention of this book is that every Christian body should examine its position in light of the six axioms which it treats. Its purpose is not to be argumentative but informative. Where it touches upon a given faith, it is for the purpose of inviting that faith's self-examination in light of these axioms. The treatment is not so much philosophical as scriptural. Its assumption is that the Bible is God's revealed word by which all systems of faith and practice should be gauged. It is presented with the hope and prayer that preconceived notions in the Christian faith will be tested by these axioms and that, where found necessary, adjustments will be made. Various systems of faith did not develop in a day. It is unlikely that they will be adjusted in a day. But perhaps these axioms may be seed sown which in time will yield a harvest.

A word is in order as to the dual nature of the authorship of this book, since Edgar Young Mullins died about a half-century ago. His book *The Axioms of Religion* was published in 1908 by the American Baptist Publication Society. But it has been out of print for many years. In my presidential address at the Southern Baptist Convention in 1962 I quoted from it. W. W. Leathers, Jr., a former seminary mate of mine, suggested that I should undertake a revision of Mullins' book. I passed the idea along to Broadman Press and received a favorable reaction. A few years later when I was ready to undertake it, the Press suggested that the revision might bear both Mullins' name and mine. In this way I would be free to use material from his original book without the necessity of quoting him. Where I have used his material, largely in the introductory portions of chapters 2–10, I have sought to preserve his meaning.

Since I am a Southern Baptist much of the treatment reflects the viewpoint which is largely held by Baptists of the world. However, it is my prayer and hope that this will not overshadow the primary purposes of the book: to enable others to get a clearer understanding of Baptists; to allow Baptists to better understand themselves; to inspire other Christian groups and individuals to examine their own faith in light of these axioms.

It is with goodwill toward all and a desire on my part to prove helpful that this book is sent forth.

HERSCHEL H. HOBBS

Oklahoma City, Oklahoma
September 1977

1 / "Who Are These Baptists, Anyway?"

The election of Jimmy Carter, a Southern Baptist, as President of the United States led multitudes of Americans to *discover* the largest evangelical body in the nation. On every hand, especially in the northern half of the United States, people were heard to ask, ''Who are these Baptists, anyway?'' To the average Baptist this may seem like a strange question. It was not a question asked in hostility but out of curiosity. One would think that Baptists are a *Johnny-come-lately* people upon the religious scene, when indeed in Europe the existence of their churches as such antedates the earliest colonists in North America. Furthermore, they played a vital role in shaping the basic elements of the United States of America. This is especially true with regard to the separation of church and state, with the subsequent result of religious freedom. While Baptists were not alone in the struggle against the principle of an established church, they were always in the vanguard of the conflict. One American historian has called religious liberty in the United States the ''trophy of the Baptists.''

Historical Survey

Baptists are sometimes accused of indulging in ''Baptist brag.'' However, one will hardly find a better and more accurate summary of Baptist history than that written by Frank S. Mead, a Methodist. The section on *The Baptists* was published under that title by Broadman Press in 1954. So as we lift certain quotes from this volume, let us permit a Methodist to do the bragging for us.

Mead begins the book thus: ''How old are the Baptists? Well, how old are the hills? One date is as hard to determine, to pin down as another.'' Noting that other denominations can date with precision their beginnings by naming a man and a place, he says that this is not true of Baptists. "There are many Democrats before Thomas Jefferson, but the Democratic *party* began with him. Just so, there were many Baptists before [John] Smyth, but their origin as a *denomination* began with him, in 1608 . . . . [The Baptist] is quite within reason in claiming that his *principles* are as old as Christ in Jordan." [1] Note that he says "principles," not an unbroken line of churches.

Mead lists these principles as baptism of believers, loyalty to the Scriptures, independence of the local church, and complete separation of church and state.

> They have never been a state church, never taken orders from any government or king [at the same time being good citizens where man's law did not conflict with God's law]; in their blood is an eternal insistence that the state shall rule only in affairs political, and let the church alone. They are God's patriots, putting allegiance to him always above allegiance to Caesar. Freedom of conscience and complete divorce of church and state! How they have suffered for that! They have faced mockery and mud, fines, whippings and iron bars; [in Europe] they have been burned at the stake and pulled on the rack, but they have held to it. And note this: *never once in their bitter, bloody history have they struck back at their persecutors or persecuted any other for his faith.* That is patriotism touched by the divine.

Mead briefly notes certain groups which intermittently held to principles now espoused by Baptists: Waldensians (from Peter Waldo), Anabaptists (rebaptizers), and Mennonites (from Menno Sims). He points out certain extremes held by some in addition to New Testament truth, extremes which Baptists do not hold. John Christian Wenger, a Mennonite, professor of theology at Goshen College Bible Seminary, and former moderator of the Mennonite General Conference, presents another side of the usual concept of Anabaptists. He shows that the traditional view of this group was "a distorted and biased portrait of the Anabaptists drawn by their opponents." But further research has shown "how devoutly these Täufer, as they were called in German, sought to follow Christ, how earnestly they loved God's Word and tried to obey it, how seriously they clung to the principle of freedom of conscience, how profoundly they opposed the principle of a state church, how vigorously they objected to binding salvation to ceremonies, and how eagerly they attempted the evangelization of Europe." [2]

But getting back to the Baptists in America. Of Roger Williams, the founder of the Rhode Island Colony on the principle of separation of church and state, Mead says that he "contributed to the making of the United States hardly less than any dozen presidents."

No more thrilling story can be found in American history than an event in the colony of Virginia. But let us let Mead the Methodist tell it as he speaks of Baptists.

> William Weber and Joseph Anthony were locked up in Chesterfield jail and told to be quiet [about the gospel]. They preached through the bars of their cells to crowds in the streets outside. John Waller, Louis Craig and James Childs were mobbed and brought into court, where a wild-eyed prosecuting attorney cried above the hubbub, "May it please your worship, these men are great disturbers of the peace; they cannot meet a man upon the road, but they must ram a text of scripture down his throat!"
>
> It looked bad for the defendants. Fifty miles away, a young Scotch-American lawyer named Patrick Henry (a good Episcopalian) heard of it, turned red to the roots of his hair, saddled his horse and galloped into town. Waving the indictment above his head in a fury wilder than that of the prosecuting attorney, he roared, "For preaching the gospel of God. Great God! Great God!! Great God!!!" . . . The preachers were acquitted.

Every schoolchild knows about Henry's "Give me liberty, or give me death." But in the annals of eternity this famous and patriotic cry must take second place to his roaring cry in the Virginia courthouse.

Citing individuals, Mead speaks of "Squire" Boone, a Baptist preacher and brother of Daniel Boone. The mother of young Abe Lincoln was a staunch Baptist, and Lincoln's father helped to build the Baptist church at Pigeon Creek. Speaking of the Baptist circuit rider he says:

> Into the wilderness, into the boisterous pandemonium of the wilderness town, rode the Baptist on horseback. Call the roll of the new states (Kentucky, Ohio, Indiana, Illinois, Texas, California, Colorado, Oregon) and find a Baptist at work preaching God and building his meetinghouse. No spot was too hard to reach; no town too tough to tackle. Was there drinking, and carousing, fighting, gambling, killing,

horse-stealing or (what was worse) horse-racing? He fought it, tempered it with his stern code, stood for law and order if he had to stand alone, took the snap, the sting, the poison out of it. When he dropped on the wilderness trail, the churches he'd left behind him carried on.

Through the years Baptists in the United States have had their share of internal problems. In 1814 they divided almost equally over the question of foreign missions. Behind this is a thrilling story. During the War of 1812 while British warships prowled the seas, two ships sailed from the United States bound for India. They carried the precious cargo of three missionaries: Adoniram Judson and his wife Ann Hasseltine Judson on one ship and Luther Rice, a bachelor, on the other. This was the direct result of the "haystack prayer meeting" at Williams College. They went out under the Congregational mission board. In anticipation of answers for English Baptists in India, the Judsons spent their long voyage studying the Greek New Testament with respect to baptism. By the time they reached India they were convinced of the truth of the Baptist position and were immersed by the English Baptists. Independently Rice had the same experience.

Since they could no longer expect support from the Congregationalists, Rice returned to America to challenge Baptists to support their work. This resulted in a division among Baptists in the United States. One group holding to strong Calvinism insisted that the *elect* would be saved, so foreign missions was unnecessary. The other group took Christ's Great Commission at face value. The former group gradually waned to the point that only a small group of them still exists. The other group flourished into several strong Baptist bodies known today.

God blesses missionary churches. George W. Truett once said, "A church that is not missionary does not deserve the ground upon which its building stands. For 'The earth is the Lord's, and the fulness thereof; the world, and they that dwell therein' (Ps. 24:1)."

The movement under Alexander Campbell, a former Baptist preacher, led multiplied thousands out of the Baptist fold. But Baptists continued to grow. In 1845 Baptists of the North and South divided over the issue of whether or not slaveholders should be appointed as foreign missionaries. Yet they continued to grow in numbers. Despite the ravages of the Civil

War by 1880, according to Mead, there were 1,672,631 Baptists in the South and over 2,500,000 in all the United States. Since that time Baptists in the South have been the largest group. In addition to the American Baptist Churches U.S.A. and the Southern Baptist Convention, there are three major conventions of black Baptists. These are numerous smaller Baptist bodies based upon various doctrinal and ethnic lines.

According to Mead, immediately after the Civil War

> the Baptists went to work to relieve the real victim of the war. That victim was the Negro.
>
> Far from being the benefactor he was intended to be, the black stood at the surrender like a youngster toying with a precious Venetian vase. He had freedom but he did not know what to do with it. Carefully, the Baptists guided him, in the finest piece of home missionary work in the annals of the church. They built schools, churches, institutions of all kinds, for his own particular benefit. Some day someone will write a great story—the story of the Christianizing of the Negro in the days of slavery and afterward. And the Baptists will be among the great heroes of the story. Education, they saw, was the remedy and the safeguard against the perils of the liberation: religious education, or education with a religious aim. They have outstripped all others in the building of colored schools; in the year of our Lord 1954, the colored [black] Baptists have a membership of over seven million with thirty-seven thousand churches.

The number is much greater in 1977. The report of the Baptist World Alliance at the Southern Baptist Convention in 1976 (see the 1976 *Annual of the Southern Baptist Convention,* pp. 243–244) shows three major black Baptist conventions with a total of 40,878 churches with a combined membership of 10,550,000. It further shows that in the United States there were at that time 28,501,041 Baptists in a total of 98,611 churches. Of this number Southern Baptists had 34,902 churches— located in every state in the Union—with a total membership of 12,735,662 (the number now exceeds the 13,000,000 mark), making it the largest non-Roman Catholic body in the nation.

One of the most thrilling stories to come out of the civil rights struggle of the 1960s was practically, if not altogether, ignored by the nonreligious news media of the nation. Its only news publicity came largely through Baptist state papers.

The news media heralded far and wide the tragic burning of black churches in Mississippi by a small group of extremists. Early one morning the man in charge of the work among the black people by the Mississippi Baptist Convention (white) sat in his car and wept as he viewed the still-smoking embers of a church building burned during the night. His mind turned to words found in Isaiah 61:3: "To give them beauty for ashes." He prayed and vowed with God's help to lead the white Baptists of Mississippi to rebuild every church building burned in that state. Mississippi Baptists rallied behind the program. As the movement became known other religious groups, including Roman Catholics and Jews, asked to be included. The result was that *every church that was burned in that state was rebuilt and furnished*. The American Bible Society gave a large pulpit Bible to each one. Truly they gave them "beauty for ashes."

Baptists have excelled in the fields of religious and Christian education—Sunday Schools and higher institutions of learning. Robert Raikes of England is usually credited with starting a school on Sunday, with paid teachers, to teach poor children in secular as well as religious subjects. But the first school in history for the study of the Bible by young people (Sunday School) was founded in 1783 in London by a wealthy Baptist deacon, William Fox. The first Sunday School in America was started in the First Baptist Church of Philadelphia in 1815. Mead wrote: "The first Sunday school paper for young people in the United States, the *Young Reaper,* was a Baptist production. So were the International Uniform Sunday School Lessons, which were the work of a Chicago layman, B. F. Jacobs."

Mead takes note of the contribution of Baptists in the field of higher education. "They have presented us with scores of colleges (Bates, Bucknell, Colby, Denison, Franklin, Vassar, Wake Forest), universities (Baylor, Brown, Colgate, Richmond), eighteen seminaries, and numerous secondary schools. They have more dollars invested in education, at the moment, than any other church in America."

Statistics Cited

But even this list is far from complete. According to the 1976 *Southern*

Baptist Convention Annual, the Baptists within the states cooperating through the Southern Baptist Convention had at that time forty-three accredited senior colleges and universities with a total enrollment of 110,861; ten junior colleges with an enrollment of 10,048; seven academies with an enrollment of over 2,963; and four Bible schools with an enrollment of 1,132. The Southern Baptist Convention itself operates six theological seminaries with a total enrollment of over 9,000 students. In addition these seminaries cooperate in the Seminary Extension Department with an enrollment of 6,702 students.

A recent secular magazine article by a non-Baptist noted that Southern Baptists alone baptize an average of eight thousand people each week. And each one of these has made a personal and responsible commitment to Jesus Christ! In the 1940s another article on Southern Baptists in a secular magazine, noting their rapid growth, called them "the miracle denomination." That they are not concerned about themselves alone is evidenced by the fact that the goal for the Cooperative Program (missionary program outside the local states) for 1977–1978 was in excess of 63 million dollars. In addition to this their special offerings for Home and Foreign Missions annually approximate half that sum. In 1975 Southern Baptists had 2,667 foreign missionaries serving in eighty-two countries. Home missionaries total 2,124. In both cases these were the largest number of missionaries under appointment by any evangelical body in the nation. Figures for other Baptist bodies are not available to the writer. But these are evidence that Baptists are a missionary people.

Being fearful of the charge of "Baptist brag," I can only quote a character, Will Sonnett, played by Walter Brennan on television. "No brag—just fact!"

In light of the facts set forth in this chapter, most of them coming from a non-Baptist, one can understand why it sounded strange to Baptist ears to hear the question "Who are these Baptists, anyway?" It suggests that they have been quite busy doing the Lord's work but have not done a very good job at public relations. Perhaps this is due to the fact that there are so many different bodies of Baptists in the United States. Of course, Billy Graham is a Baptist, specifically a Southern Baptist. He has preached the gospel to more people than any other man who ever lived. For this very reason his Baptist background has been swallowed up in the feeling that he belongs to Christians everywhere.

Obviously this question was asked in various parts of the nation where Baptists are not so numerous as in the South. But even there it has not been so many years since the following mistaken concept of Baptists was expressed. John Jeter Hurt, Sr. told me this story many years ago.

He was on a committee appointed by the Southern Baptist Convention to select a site in New Orleans for the location of Baptist Bible Institute, now the New Orleans Baptist Theological Seminary. The committtee selected the site of the former campus of Sophia Newcomb College. They needed thirty-two thousand dollars with which to purchase it. So they went to a New Orleans banker to arrange for a loan. They told him they wanted to start a school for the purpose of training Baptist preachers. He replied, ''We'll be glad to let you have the loan. The property is worth far more than that. But what I can't understand is why you would invest this much money in a school to train black preachers.'' His only contact with Baptists was with black Baptists who were baptizing people up and down the bayous of southern Louisiana.

Praise the Lord that they were! But the banker was to learn that these were only one group of people called Baptists. To show the progress made in that city, today if you tell any taxi driver in New Orleans that you want to go to the New Orleans Baptist Theological Seminary, the Southern Baptist Hospital, the First Baptist Church, or almost any other Baptist church, he will know how to get there. In my judgment this change has been brought about by these institutions and the ministry of J. D. Grey, who for over thirty-five years as pastor of the First Baptist Church was known as ''Mr. Baptist'' in New Orleans. Other Baptist pastors and leaders are involved in the total life of the city.

Migration of People

Another factor affecting not only Baptists but all non-Catholics was their migration to the Gulf Coast during World War II. Since this area was originally settled by French and Spanish people, it had always been overwhelmingly Roman Catholic. But during the war this picture changed as non-Catholic people from inland moved to the Gulf Coast to work in war industries. Several years later the non-Catholics employed a firm to take a religious census of New Orleans. Everyone was surprised to learn the result—48 percent Catholic, 52 percent non-Catholic. While no other census was taken, this reflects the general change in such places as Mobile, Alabama.

I was on the board of trustees of New Orleans Baptist Theological Seminary when a larger campus became necessary. Only one large tract of land was for sale on the same side of the river. One day after a vote of the trustees the seminary president, Roland Q. Leavell, bought the choice portion of this tract, paying the cash price of 200,000 dollars. It happened that the archbishop wanted this same land for developing a Catholic residential area and building a cathedral. He was quite surprised the next day when his representatives, sent to purchase it, reported that the previous day the seminary had bought it and had *paid cash* for it. It was quite evident that the Baptists had arrived, along with a host of other non-Catholics.

During this same migration many Southern Baptists went north and west. They began to organize churches of their own. Soon they were petitioning to be received as conventions into the Southern Baptist Convention fellowship. Many years before such had happened in southern Illinois. But at the 1942 Convention in San Antonio, Texas, California Southern Baptists were received into the Convention. This marked a major step in Southern Baptists' change from a sectional to a national body. Gradually they have spread to all the states, including Alaska and Hawaii. At first other Baptist groups regarded them as rivals. Today for the most part they are welcomed as fellow laborers in a task too big for all of us.

Baptists in the Spotlight

Why this sudden interest in Baptists? As stated earlier, it was aroused largely by the election of a Southern Baptist president, Jimmy Carter. Two other Baptists have occupied the White House (Warren G. Harding and Harry S Truman). But the religious impact of candidate Jimmy Carter was most evident when in a press conference he stated that he was a "born-again Christian." This sent the news media on a flurry of research to learn what this term meant. This one statement caught the public attention more than the multiplied thousands of sermons preached by Baptist preachers on "Ye must be born again." Danger signals soon appeared as commercial enterprises sought to cash in on the term: One could be "born again" by buying this or that product. But the statement of candidate Carter soon became a part of the popular American vocabulary—especially after his election to the presidency. A nationwide television network documentary, "Born Again," avows this fact. No doubt Carter is not the first "born-again" president we have had. But he was the first one to openly declare that fact to the news media. Some even questioned if this statement would not become a political liability. But apparently it has not.

On the day of Carter's inauguration at a private worship service for the new president and vice-president and their families and members of the cabinet and their families, the preacher of the occasion was Nelson Price, pastor of the Roswell Street Baptist Church, Marietta, Georgia. The news media reported that he had been the president's "prayer partner" for many years—a fact that shows that Carter has been an active Baptist layman through the years.

So the nation found that it had a new phenomenon on its hands. Who can estimate the value for Sunday School of the television publicity concerning the First Family's arrival at church on the first Sunday after the inauguration? With his large Bible under his arm, the president replied yes to a newsman's question as to whether or not he had studied his lesson. Later in the class a friend of mine reported that he gave evidence that he had. The teacher, Fred Gregg, began by asking what the topic of the previous Sunday's lesson had been. When no one replied, he repeated the question. President Carter quietly said, "The parable of the good Samaritan." When in the city he teaches this class twice a month. He had been a deacon and the regular teacher of a men's class in the Baptist church of Plains, Georgia. According to the pastor, Charles A. Trentham, the regular teacher of the class travels at times because of his business. When he called the president to fill in for him "because of the teacher's busy schedule," Mr. Carter agreed, saying he was "always glad to help a busy man."

At the morning worship service the president and his family joined the First Baptist Church, Washington, D.C. by letter from the Plains Baptist Church. The First Baptist Church is dually aligned with both the Southern Baptist Convention and the American Baptist Churches U.S.A. Amy Carter made her public profession of faith.

The week before Amy was baptized Trentham had calls from around the nation. "They asked why she was not baptized as an infant." This was from newsmen who were "not religiously oriented." When Trentham baptized Amy, the secret service man assigned to guard her became nervous. He asked an usher what the pastor was doing and if it was dangerous. [3] The next day the Oklahoma City *Daily Oklahoman* carried a front page wire story under a large headline. It explained in detail the meaning and method of baptism as practiced by Baptists. I presume that other newspapers carried the story. If so, the general reading public more than ever before learned of New Testament baptism as practiced by Baptists.

It is reported that President Carter has two hot lines in the Oval Office—one to the Kremlin and one to his pastor's study. The pastor says that he has never used it. But the president has done so, for reasons such as to explain why he will not be in Sunday School and the church worship service when his presidential duties take him out of Washington on any given Sunday.

Opportunity and Responsibility

Is it any wonder, then, that people unfamiliar with Baptists suddenly began to wonder what kind of people they are? This presented an *opportunity* for them to show people who and what they are, not only across the nation but within the locality of their churches. And this posed a greater responsibility for Baptists to be bold in the proclamation of their witness for Christ. Popular curiosity could result in false answers to the question "Who are these Baptists, anyway?" Claiming to be a people of Christ, they must follow his example in caring for people not only through a social program but also in a renewed dedication to the commission of Christ to disciple all nations both at home and around the world. The fish bowl position into which they were thrust called for more than a business-as-usual policy. It should thrust them out into a bold mission for our Lord.

This question also calls upon Baptists to ask the question "Who are we, anyway?" Do we really understand ourselves? Are we really Baptistic in our relations to one another and to other Christians? What are the basic principles that characterize us as a people? How do we relate to the larger Christian family in other denominations? What is the historical significance of Baptists? What self-evident truths are the warp and woof of our faith and practice? The following chapters will seek to answer these questions.

Notes

[1] Frank S. Mead, *See These Banners Go* (New York: The Bobbs-Merrill Company, 1936). All succeeding quotations from Mead not otherwise footnoted are taken from this book.

[2] John Christian Wenger, *Even Unto Death* (Richmond: John Knox Press, 1961), p. 7.

2 / Baptists and Denominationalism

Whether one accepts or deplores the fact, denominationalism seems to be the widely accepted pattern of modern Christianity. It would be an anachronism to speak of denominations in terms of the first century, for such did not exist at that time. Denominations in the modern sense date from the time of the Protestant Reformation. It may surprise some people to note that the New Testament term is not *denomination* but *ecumenical*. The latter word is the anglicized form of the Greek word *oikoumene*, which means the inhabited earth—so worldwide, universal, or general.

This is not a plea for this term as used by many people today. It simply recognizes a fact of Christian history. But when Jesus prayed in John 17:11,21 he did not ask that his followers *become* one, but that they "may be one" or "may continue to be one." He prayed that the oneness of his followers in faith, fellowship, and purpose would continue. And he visualized such a fellowship of faith and purpose on a worldwide basis as seen in his various commissions (cf. Matt. 28:18–20; Acts 1:8). However, it was to be based upon a fellowship of spirit and truth, not upon mechanical expediency. It is precisely at this point that Jesus' concept differs from that held by many Christians today. New Testament truth is the sole basis for unity (not organic union) and cooperation between the various Christian bodies.

Tares Among the Wheat

The roots of denominationalism are found in the New Testament itself. The New Testament presents the clear and full revelation of God in Jesus Christ. But by the middle of the first century the devil had sown tares among the wheat of divine truth. These tares consisted largely of

25

elements of Greek philosophy, Judaism, and Oriental mysticism.

One of these tares was based upon pagan philosophy. For instance, in 1 Corinthians 15 Paul opposed the basic philosophy of Plato. Plato taught that spirit is abiding, but matter is temporal. Thus his philosophy was inherently a denial of the bodily resurrection. The spirit lives on, he said, but the body perishes. This position is in direct contradiction of New Testament teachings concerning both Jesus' bodily resurrection and that of his people. Incidentally, this view of Plato denied the meaning of the Greek word for *resurrection*, "a standing again"; something which died lives again to die no more. Since the spirit does not die, it can refer only to the body.

Another tare was Gnosticism. This was a philosophy made up of elements of Judaism, pagan philosophy, and the Oriental mystery religions. It sought to explain the origin of the universe. Holding that God is absolutely good and matter is absolutely evil, its problem was to explain how such a God could create an evil universe. To solve the problem the Gnostics imagined a series of created beings coming out of God in descending order, each possessing less deity than the one above it. The lowest being in the chain possessed enough deity to create but so little as to be able to create only evil matter. When the Gnostics came into contact with Christianity, they identified Christ as this lowest being. Thus they regarded him as a created being, a demigod, and almost a demon since he created evil matter.

Concerning Christ the Gnostics were divided into two groups. The Docetics (from the Greek verb *dokeō,* I seem) said that Christ did not have a real flesh-and-blood body, but only *seemed* to have. Thus they denied the humanity of Christ. The Cerinthians (from their leader Cerinthus) held that Christ was neither born nor died. The role of Christ came upon Jesus at his baptism and left him on the cross. This view denied the deity of Jesus. Obviously this system cut at the very heart of Christian truth concerning Jesus Christ.

Because of their distinction between the nature of God and of evil matter, the Gnostics divided into two other groups. One group withdrew altogether from the world in order to save their souls. The other group said that since there was no relationship between body and spirit, what the body practiced did not affect the soul. This resulted in riotous living. These views were the seeds which later in Christianity bore the respective harvests of asceticism and antinomianism. The former produced monasticism in place of evangelism; the latter produced carnal (flesh-controlled) rather than spiritual (Spirit-controlled) Christians (1 Cor. 3:1–3). Multitudes through the ages have crucified Christian virtues on the cross of pagan philosophy.

We see apostolic opposition to this philosophy especially in Colossians, the Gospel of John, and 1 John (John 1:1–3,14; 10:30; Col. 1:15–17,20; 2:9; 1 John 1:1; 2:18–19,22–23; 4:1–3; 5:20). Paul called it a philosophy derived from human tradition and one characterized by empty deceit (Col. 2:8).

A third tare was the teaching of the Judaizers (Acts 15:1). These were Jewish Christians who still insisted that salvation was for Jews only. For a Gentile to be saved he must become a Jewish proselyte through circumcision, certain other religious rites, and living by the Mosaic law. Then he must believe in Jesus as Savior. This was a system of works plus faith, in direct contrast to the gospel of salvation by grace through faith as preached by Paul and others (Acts 15:11; Eph. 2:8–10).

The Jerusalem Conference (Acts 15; Gal. 2) was held to decide this issue. It decided in favor of a gospel of salvation by grace through faith. But the Judaizers continued to teach their heresy, including attacks upon Paul's apostleship and personal character. Furthermore, largely through their opposition to Gentile missions, the Jerusalem church as a body never really responded to the Great Commission. The center of Christian influence shifted to Antioch. The Jerusalem church was never a potent instrument of the Lord in the spread of the gospel beyond Palestine. With the fall of Jerusalem in A.D. 70 it disappeared. This church, like so many since, committed suicide, strangled to death by legalism and ritualism. It began so grandly but ended so miserably. And it stands as a warning to churches and denominations through the ages, even today.

Galatians is Paul's direct onslaught against the Judaizers. This controversy is also reflected in most of Paul's other writings, especially in the Corinthian epistles. Some of his most excoriating words were directed against them in Galatians 1:6–9.

Unfortunately these tares still grow among the wheat. And as in Jesus' parable, it is often difficult to differentiate between the two. The modern tares are not really advanced thinkers. Those who deny the bodily resurrection teach Neoplatonism. Those who deny the humanity of Christ and/or the deity of Jesus and who either retire from the world or else embrace its pagan values parrot neo-Gnosticism. And those who in any form add works to faith as a necessity for redemption are neo-Judaizers. We may not be able to separate the tares from the wheat. But every Christian and every separate Christian body should be on guard against becoming infected by the tares. Since only God can judge righteously, we should ever be aware that we are personally responsible before him.

Scripture Versus Tradition

Another element that contributed to the perversion of New Testament truth and ultimately to denominationalism was the growth of traditions contrary to divine revelation. Jesus himself condemned the Jewish scribes and Pharisees for setting aside the clear teachings of Old Testament Scripture in favor of their traditions (Mark 7:1–13). But the same vicious practice soon crept into New Testament Christianity. Jesus never disobeyed a law of God, but he vigorously opposed human tradition which perverted divine revelation. And he taught his disciples to be on the lookout for and "beware of the leaven [doctrine, Matt. 16:12] of the Pharisees and the Sadducees" (Matt. 16:6).

A tradition (*paradosis*) is a belief or practice handed down from one person or generation to another. It may be either good or bad, according to its nature. In 1 Corinthians 11:2 where the word is rendered "ordinances" (KJV) Paul used it in the good sense of Christian teachings. But in Colossians 2:5 he used it in the bad sense in reference to the Gnostic heresy.

The Roman Catholic Church openly claims two sources of authority: the Scriptures and tradition. But it holds that tradition is of greater value. Traditions in this sense began early in the second century. But they took years, in some cases centuries, to develop into their present form. Repeated practice gradually gained them respectability, then acceptance; and in some cases they became dogmas of the church. A dogma is a pronouncement by a council and later by the pope speaking *ex cathedra* (from his *seat* as pope and said to be by divine revelation) which Catholics must believe in order to be saved.

For instance, to see how tradition develops, take the matter of baptism. New Testament scholarship agrees that immersion was the form of baptism used in the first century.[1] It was symbolic in nature. And it was for believers only or for those who were capable of making a conscious and personal decision to receive Jesus Christ as Savior. No Bible scholar endeavors to justify infant baptism on scriptural grounds. As simple as this practice may seem to the casual observer, it has been the principal means whereby multitudes of churches have become plagued with unregenerated people in their midst. The statistics of the high percentage of church members and the very low percentage of those attending church services in some European nations—plus the low standards of morals—may be primarily attributed to infant baptism, which involves no spiritual change in human nature. But as belief in baptismal regeneration began in the second century (here was works plus faith), it led to the baptism of infants [2] and clinical baptism for the seriously ill.

This soon led to pouring for baptism. The earliest mention of pouring as a permitted form of baptism is found in the *Teaching of the Twelve Apostles,* a noncanonical work which probably dates back to the former half of the second century. This eventually led to the more convenient form of sprinkling. The New Testament has Greek words for pouring and sprinkling, but they are never used in connection with baptism.

By the thirteenth century sprinkling had become the norm in the Roman Catholic Church. Roman Catholic scholars readily admit that baptism in the New Testament was by immersion, but that their Church changed the form to sprinkling. Of course, through the centuries some dissenting groups continued to immerse believers only.

Believer's baptism is by no means a panacea for correcting all social and spiritual illness, as may be seen in the unfortunate track record even among Baptists. But in all fairness we should recognize the pagan social climate produced by unregenerated people, to which many regenerated people, Baptists and others, have succumbed. Furthermore, those who preach and teach that one must be born from above before he can enter the kingdom of God, others as well as Baptists, are the more evangelistic and missionary groups.

Even at the lower level of self-preservation those who believe in believer's baptism must be more evangelistic. They do not add new members by way of the baptismal font and catechism class, but by following believer's baptism resulting from a personal encounter and experience with Christ.

Tradition rather than Scripture developed the hierarchical system of the Roman Church. Gradually following the political pattern of the Roman empire, the simple New Testament pattern of pastors and deacons, congregational government, and local church autonomy was expanded into a complex system of graded priestly orders. To note the correspondence of the ecclesiastical to the political pattern note: pope and emperor; cardinals and senate; archbishops and provincial governors or propraetors; bishops and tetrarchs, rulers of a fourth of a territory under the authority of the provincial governors; local priests and local officials.

Power gradually centered in the pastors or bishops of key churches in the empire. Since the empire's power centered in Rome, the Roman bishop eventually emerged as the highest ecclesiastical power. Innocent I (402–417) was the first bishop of Rome to claim universal jurisdiction based upon the tradition that Peter was the first bishop of Rome for twenty-five years. According to Robert Baker this tradition came much later; and according to outstanding Roman Catholic writers this claim can never be proved. [3] Baker also notes that Leo I (440–461) "may rightly be called the first pope." [4] He based his claim upon three passages of Scripture (Matt. 16:18–19; Luke 22:31–32; John 21:15–17), all of which better lend themselves to quite a different interpretation. It should also be noted that when the emperor Constantine, who called himself "bishop of bishops," moved his capital city to Byzantium (Constantinople, now Istanbul) a power vacuum was created in the West which the bishop of Rome filled. This enabled him to develop his claim of supremacy without restraint. He "became both ecclesiastical and secular sovereign. The Roman bishops became administrators of the secular affairs of the city, defending it against military aggressors, maintaining internal order, supplying its physical needs, and initiating its foreign policy." [5]

This led ultimately to the claims of Innocent I and Leo I. The latter "was able to dictate the doctrinal statement of the Council of Chalcedon, the fourth universal council in 451. 'Peter has spoken,' cried the bishops when Leo's Tome was read; and such recognition, imperial and ecclesiastical, laid the foundations of the papal system." [6] The hierarchical system reached its climax at the Vatican Council in 1870 when it declared as a dogma the infallibility of the pope when he speaks *ex cathedra*.

But it should be recognized that this was the fruit of tradition, not Scripture. As far as explicit New Testament teaching is concerned, there are no important points left unsettled among scholars as to the organization and polity of the church. Men do not hesitate, however, to neglect New Testament teaching on these points in the interest of a theory of development or for other reasons when it suits their purposes, and they seek to justify the procedure in many ways.

Mariolatry is another product of tradition. According to Hastings' *Dictionary of the Bible* the earliest mention of its beginnings is found in a reference by Epiphanius (A.D. 370). He referred to heretics called Collyridians, who worshiped the virgin Mary. This early practice seems to have been grounded in the pagan worship of the "queen of heaven" (Jer. 7:17–18). Epiphanius strongly rebuked them. But it was not long before the practice was accepted in the church. Mary was given the title Theotokos and finally was called both "Mother of God" and "Queen of Heaven."

In the process she was said to be sinless. This gave rise to the dogma of the Immaculate Conception (that Mary was conceived without sin) declared by Pope Pius IX in 1854. For centuries the "Assumption of Mary" was taught—that is, that at her death her body was taken immediately into heaven. But in recent years another dogma was handed down by the pope to the effect that she went to heaven without dying! Instead of praying directly to God in Jesus' name, prayer was/is made to Mary that she will intercede with her Son Jesus on behalf of the suppliant.

In Michelangelo's *Last Judgment* in the Sistine Chapel of the Vatican, God the Father is placed at the top. Immediately below him sits Jesus on his throne. And beside him sits Mary on hers. Thus practically every attribute of Jesus Christ is given to Mary, with one striking addition. He died and rose again before ascending into heaven. She now is said to have gone to heaven without dying! Mariolatry presents quite a different picture of Mary than the one found in the New Testament. This is one striking example of what can happen when one gives tradition an authority greater than that of the Scriptures.

Many other such examples could be cited—such as the Mass in contrast to the beautiful and symbolic Lord's Supper. But these are sufficient to demonstrate the point of departing from the revelation of God recorded in the New Testament in favor of the traditions of men. Once one departs from the New Testament as the one authority in Christian belief and practice, he becomes a potential victim of every kind of distortion and error.

Rise of Denominationalism

Thus we see the basis for the rise of denominationalism. During the centuries when basic Christian faith and practice were being corrupted, some minority groups continued to hold to the truth of the New Testament with certain variations. Persecution drove them underground, but they appeared at intervals under different names as noted in chapter 1. The best known of these groups were the Anabaptists, who were found mainly in Germany and Switzerland. Church historians for the most part agree that they derived their beliefs from some of the other aforementioned groups. These are the immediate ancestors of the Baptists. The prefix *ana* was dropped eventually, leaving *Baptist*.

H. C. Vedder says of the Anabaptists at the time of the Protestant Reformation:

> "Abundant documentary proofs exist to show that they were numerous, widespread, and indefatigable; that their chief men were not

> inferior in learning and eloquence to any of the reformers; that their teachings were scriptural, consistent, and moderate, except where persecution produced the usual result of enthusiasm and vagary . . . these Anabaptists were not gradually developed, but appear fully formed from the first—complete in polity, sound in doctrine, strict in discipline. It will be found impossible to account for these phenomena without an assumption of a long-existing cause. Though the Anabaptist churches appear suddenly in the records of time, contemporaneously with the Zwinglian Reformation, their roots are to be sought farther back." [7]

Significant is the fact that Vedder divides his book into two sections: "History of Baptist Principles" and "A History of Baptist Churches." The latter begins with 1610.

From this brief examination of the rise of Baptists and the principles held by them, it is evident that there is substance behind the modern claim that Baptists are not Protestants in the classical sense of that term. However, it is recognized that they are popularly classified as evangelicals with other groups in contradistinction to Roman Catholicism. But no matter how one classifies Baptists they do constitute a denomination. In the *Encyclopedia of Southern Baptists,* C. Earl Cooper defines a denomination as "those who are bound together by a large measure of agreement with regard to doctrines and polity and by a desire for co-operation among the various churches holding to these tenets." [8] And though the history of an unbroken line of Baptist churches dates back to early in the seventeenth century, their emergence as such is related to the general spirit of reform in the sixteenth century.

We must distinguish between a denomination and conventions. As previously noted, there are many conventions of Baptists in the United States—as well as throughout the world. But Baptists everywhere comprise the denomination.

Looking at the larger field of Christendom, in terms of other modern major denominations, we see that the Reformation produced such groups as Lutherans, Presbyterians, and the Church of England or Episcopalians. The first two resulted from religious reforms in Germany and Switzerland. The last was the result of a break between Henry VIII and the Vatican. Later the Methodist denomination began as a movement resulting from the Church of England's refusal to permit John Wesley to preach in their churches. In the United States the Disciples of Christ (Christian Church) and the Church of Christ were the result of a break between the Baptists and Alexander Campbell, brought about when Campbell began to preach baptismal regeneration. He and his followers retained the New Testament mode of immersion but changed the meaning from a symbol to a sacrament or as possessing saving quality.

But looking at the denominations which were the immediate result of the Reformation, one thing is evident. It is a truism that you can come out of a river, but you bring some of the river out with you. Thus in various ways these denominations reflect some modified form of Roman Catholicism such as sprinkling for baptism, infant baptism, and varying forms of ecclesiology. In the Church of England the archbishop of Canterbury simply replaced the pope. The High Church in England is sometimes referred to as the English Catholic Church.

Beginning with the Reformation, denominationalism was characterized by conflict both intellectual and violent. While they have never persecuted others, Baptists have often been persecuted both in Europe and America. But violence finally gave way to doctrinal disputes and debates. However, debates between denominations largely lost favor in the first quarter of the twentieth century.

During the 1920s conflict was largely within denominations as the Modernist Controversy reached a climax. Divisions occurred in some denominations. Many were largely swept from their traditionally conservative moorings. Perhaps the most potent force in holding Southern Baptists to their traditional conservative theological position was the adoption in 1925 of *The Baptist Faith and Message*. It is not a creed to which a Southern Baptist must adhere. This statement declared the freedom of the individual conscience, but set forth the basic doctrinal position generally held by Southern Baptists. During another doctrinal controversy a revised form of this statement was adopted in 1963. It continues to serve as a steadying force for this body. At the present time divisions have taken place or seem possible among Presbyterians and Missouri Synod Lutherans. These conditions seem for the most part to be doctrinal in nature.

Some denominations endeavor to trace their origin to New Testament times. But even if this were possible, the important thing is not to trace an unbroken line of churches back to the first century. Rather, the vital thing is how nearly a given denominational body today adheres to divine truth as revealed and recorded in the New Testament. For the sake of brevity only a few examples of departure from this truth have been cited. No one group can claim a corner on all truth. Only Jesus is the Truth. The test of denominations, therefore, is to determine the degree of faithfulness to this truth. Baptists welcome a comparison at this point.

The Ecumenical Movement

No treatment of denominations can ignore this movement. As controversies between denominations waned, a movement in the opposite direction arose—the modern ecumenical movement. As noted previously the word *ecumenical* is not new in Christian thought. Long before the Reformation it was used for the gathering of Christian leaders for various councils. In the Protestant sense "to some extent, ecumenicalism rooted in the burst of enthusiasm for world missions [a movement begun by William Carey, who was an English Baptist]. The London Missionary Society of 1795 was made up of members from the Church of England, Scottish Presbyterians, Methodists, and Independents." [9] Efforts in this direction continued through the nineteenth century. According to W. R. Estep, Jr. the modern ecumenical movement was born in the Edinburgh Conference in 1910. [10] Here for the first time a conference was held which was composed of officially delegated representatives from mission boards and societies. This was followed by other such gatherings through the years. Eventually in 1948 in Amsterdam, the World Council of Churches was formed. However, prior to this various forces in this direction were active in North America. These resulted in the organization of the Federal National Council of Churches of Christ in America (now The National Council of Churches) in 1908, two years prior to the Edinburgh conference. Many Baptist bodies are involved in both the National and/or World Councils.

But Southern Baptists, Missouri Synod Lutherans, fundamentalists groups, and Roman Catholics have not been a part of either.

Among the reasons behind the ecumenical movement Baker lists the following: a desire for unity; the uniting of "family denominations"; the challenge of the mission field and the desire to present a united Christendom before a pagan world; the sweeping humanitarian movements; the desire for efficiency; the need for a non-Catholic united front to match the organizational unity of the Roman Catholic Church; and the effect of liberal theology, where the toning down or denial of traditional Christian convictions makes lesser denominational distinctions seem relatively academic.[11] It should be noted, however, that within the World Council of Churches goals range all the way from simple unity in a loose federation to organic union of all Christian bodies in one worldwide, visible church organization.

Southern Baptists' refusal to participate in the ecumenical movement is not due to an avowed purpose of isolation. In most cases churches cooperate with those of other denominations at the local level in matters of mutual concern which do not compromise their doctrinal position. Some local churches cooperate with various agencies of the National and World Councils. But as a body the Southern Baptist Convention has respectfully declined to become an integral part of the overall ecumenical movement.

Their position is based upon three basic principles: (1) unique doctrinal beliefs; (2) congregational church polity; and (3) practical matters such as the comity agreement, which seeks to regulate where a given denomination may or may not locate churches. It is not necessary to deal with these matters at length. But if you except 1 and 3, 2 would make it impossible for Southern Baptists to belong, say, to the National Council of Churches. That body accepts only *conventions,* not churches, into membership. The Southern Baptist Convention can take no action which binds local churches.

In recent years Pope John XXIII called a Catholic ecumenical council which met in Rome. This produced a broader understanding between Roman Catholics and non-Roman Catholics. Following that council I conducted one funeral and performed two weddings involving Roman

Catholics; each time a Catholic priest assisted in a lesser role. This was an unheard-of experience before that time. One evidence of this new attitude was seen in Billy Graham's crusade held in the football stadium at Notre Dame University in 1977. This indicates, according to *Christianity Today,* "that many elements in the once-hostile Catholic community are now receptive to Graham's type of ministry." [12] The final rally of the crusade attracted approximately forty-five thousand people. This article reports that "one priest who attended in clerical garb removed his collar as he came forward at the invitation. When the counsellor asked if he intended to rededicate his life to Christ, he insisted that he was receiving Christ as Saviour and Lord for the first time."

However, "Roman Catholic leaders maintained a low profile." The president of the university ate lunch with Billy Graham one time, but did not appear publicly with him. He sent a representative to welcome the crowd in the stadium—at the final service. "His clerical collar was one of the very few in evidence during the crusade."

While the Vatican Council did produce a better understanding, perhaps the major thrust was an invitation for other Christians to *return* to the fold of the Church on its terms. Possibly the overwhelming response to this invitation by Baptists is that in terms of New Testament truth they have not been *away.*

At the moment of this writing the one continuing ecumenical effect is a dialogue between the Vatican and the Church of England. A news release dated January 18, 1977, under the dateline of Vatican City, reported that the stage had been reached where a joint high-level commission of both Catholic and Anglican scholars proposed to recommend that the pope be recognized as overall patriarch as a means of ending the 443-year-old schism. This recommendation, according to the commission, was based upon a recognition of papal supremacy because among Christian churches only the church of Rome claims and exercises universal supremacy. Following a recent conference between the pope and the archbishop of Canterbury, it was announced that should the Church of England *return* it would be on this basis. Rome may *bend* but she never *changes*!

Elsewhere in Christendom at this time (1977) the ecumenical movement seems to be on the decline. Through the years Southern Baptists have been called the problem child of American Protestantism. But it has been my experience that the denominations which have been most vocal and insistent for ecumenicalism at the national and international levels have been the problem children concerning cooperation at the local level. For instance, in almost a half-century in the ministry the only church building in which I was refused the right to pray publicly at its altar was such a church. I record this with no malice, but to make a point. This denomination did not accept my ordination. Incidentally, this is one of the major obstacles to church union on the part of those who promote it. The wave of the moment seems to be denomination centered. This calls for each group to pursue its aims in its own way, with cooperation in matters of mutual concern that does not compromise the elements of faith held by participating bodies. It challenges each group to a greater commitment within denominations to the mission involved in the Great Commission. It should also lead each group to examine its position in light of New Testament truth.

Baptists and Ecumenicalism

One Baptist would be presuming if he undertook to speak for all other Baptists. But history does permit certain conclusions. As noted previously, each Baptist convention has determined its own relationship to the various ecumenical bodies. However, Baptists generally believe in Christian unity but not in organic church union. The latter will not meet the deepest needs of this or any other time, since it calls for all participants to renounce doctrinal beliefs dear to their hearts. Outward bigness is not enough. At a time when for all practical purposes, except for some dissenters, there was one church body, it was filled with corruption and helped to produce the Dark Ages. What is needed is an inner unity of spirit and purpose, with a full commitment to New Testament truth, as Christians confront the evangelistic, missionary, and social needs of the world.

Jesus' twice-repeated prayer for oneness in John 17 did not envision the eleven apostles becoming one man with the size and strength of eleven men. He prayed for a unity of spirit, truth, and purpose among them as that existing in the Father and the Son. Essentially God is one. But outwardly he manifests himself as Father, Son, and Spirit. In all three manifestations he is dedicated to the redemption of all people who believe in his Son as Savior.

It is this unity toward which all of God's people should strive. Ecumenicalism in terms of organic union has proved to be impractical, perhaps impossible. Whatever evils there are in denominationalism, they are not as evil as a renunciation of New Testament truth, faith, love, purpose, and spirit.

Baptists of the world cooperate in a loosely organized but deeply spiritual unity through the Baptist World Alliance. At its founding Congress in London in 1905, the preacher of the Congress sermon was A. H. Strong, prominent American Baptist theologian. Stressing the unity among world Baptists, he said, "We are bound together by our allegiance to a common Redeemer, our belief in His authoritative Word, and our sense of obligation to preach His gospel. In minor matters of faith and practice we may differ. But we have one Lord, one faith, one baptism. Not the things that divide, but the things that unite will properly engage our attention." But Strong also extended the hand of friendship to all true believers.

> It is surely our duty to confess everywhere and always that we are first Christians, and only secondly Baptists. The tie which binds us to Christ is more important in our eyes than that which binds us to those of the same faith and order. We live in hope that the Spirit of Christ in us, and in all Christian bodies, may induce such growth of mind and heart that the sense of unity in Christ may not only overtop and hide the fences of division, but may ultimately do away with these fences altogether.[13]

Strong spoke the feeling of most Baptists—not doctrinal compromise for the sake of organic union, but a call to loyalty to truth as one sees it and a spirit of Christian unity made possible through a common love for and loyalty to Christ. He spoke prophetically. For such unity seems to be the wave of the future. His words should be placed alongside those attributed to John Wesley. "If thy heart be as my heart, give me thy hand."

Notes

[1] See A. T. Robertson's "Baptism," *The International Standard Bible Encyclopaedia* 1 (Grand Rapids: William B. Eerdmans, 1949), pp. 385–388.

[2] The Baptistery in Florence, Italy, has an above-floor pool for immersion of adults, with a small pool built on one corner which is used for the immersion of infants. This building antedates the time when sprinkling became the accepted form of baptism. It also contains a mural of John immersing Jesus.

[3] Robert Baker, *A Summary of Christian History* (Nashville: Broadman Press, 1959), p. 74.

[4] Ibid., p. 73.

[5] Ibid., p. 74.

[6] Ibid., p. 73.

[7] H. C. Vedder, *A Short History of the Baptists* (Philadelphia: American Baptist Publication Society, 1907), p. 130.

[8] C. Earl Cooper, *Encylopedia of Southern Baptists* 1 (Nashville: Broadman Press, 1958), p. 360.

[9] Baker, p. 336.

[10] *Encyclopedia of Southern Baptists* 1, p. 386.

[11] Baker, p. 360.

[12] *Christianity Today,* 3 June 1977, p. 30.

[13] Quoted by Herschel H. Hobbs, "The Revelance of Our Faith as Revealed in Baptist World Congress Preaching," *Baptists of the World, 1905–1970* (Fort Worth: Southern Baptist Radio and Television Commission, 1970), p. 94.

3 / The Historical Significance of Baptists

Baptists have a noble history. And it is fitting to ask certain questions about them. What is their historical significance? What can they claim as their reason for being? Have they made any distinctive contribution to the religious life and thought of mankind? In what way have they affected religious history positively as has no other body? Before we can answer these questions it is necessary to note certain principles that are generally associated with Baptists.

Baptists certainly have a consistent record. In their advocacy of soul freedom in its completest measure and of the principle of the separation of church and state, and in their insistence upon believer's baptism and a regenerated church membership, as a group they have stood as stalwarts through the centuries. All of these are related to soul freedom and/or the individual's direct relation to God, which is at the very heart of Baptist faith and practice.

Struggle for Religious Liberty

With regard to the principle of soul liberty and the separation of church and state, they have so far outstripped all other religious bodies in modern times that without doubt the impartial historian in the future, as in the past, will accord to them the palm of leadership.

We have noted previously that Vedder divided his book into the history of Baptist principles and the history of Baptist churches. The latter dates from 1610 and a small body of believers under the leadership of John Smyth. This group was made up of English people who fled to Holland to escape persecution. Smyth and his group sought admission to the Amsterdam Waterlander Church, a Mennonite group. This was delayed until after Smyth's death in 1612. Thereafter his group drew up a confession of faith consisting of one hundred articles. William L. Lumpkin calls this "an important landmark" which may have helped in finally accomplishing union with the Mennonites in 1615.[1]

Significant is the fact that Article 84 reads, "That the magistrate is not by virtue of his office to meddle with religion, or matters of conscience, to force or compel men to this or that form of religion, or doctrine: but to leave Christian religion free, to every man's conscience, and to handle only civil transgressions (Rom. xiii), injuries and wrongs of man to man, in murder, adultery, theft, etc., for Christ only is the king, and lawgiver of the church and conscience (James iv. 12)."[2] In their first Confessions of Faith in England in the seventeenth century this principle was clearly and distinctly avowed.

Article LI of the London Confession of 1644 of the Particular Baptists (who held that Christ died only for the *elect,* so for particular ones) contains the words: "But if God with-hold the Magistrates allowance and furtherance therein [religious freedom]; yet we must . . . walk in obedience to Christ in the profession and holding forth this faith before mentioned, even in the midst of all trialls and afflictions, not accounting our goods, lands, wives, children, fathers, mothers, brethren, sisters, yea, and our own lives dear unto us, so we may finish our course with joy: remembering always we ought to obey God rather than men."[3]

In 1660 the General Baptists of England (who believed that Christ died for all men) drew up what is called "The Standard Confession." Article XXIV reads: "That it is the will, and mind of God . . . that all men should have the free liberty of their own consciences in matters of Religion, or Worship, without the least oppression, or persecution, as simply upon that account; and that for any in Authority otherwise to act, we believe is expressly contrary to the mind of Christ."[4]

Article XXV speaks of the proper duty of magistrates, then adds: "But in case the Civil Powers do, or shall at any time impose things about matters of Religion, which we through conscience to God cannot actually obey, then we with Peter also do say, that we ought (in such cases) to obey God rather than men; Acts 5:29, and accordingly do hereby declare our whole, and holy intent and purpose that (through the help of grace we will not yield, nor (in such cases) in the least actually obey them; yet humbly purposing (in the Lord's strength) patiently to suffer whatsoever shall be inflicted upon us, for our conscionable forbearance.'' [5]

John Bunyan spent more than twelve years in a Bedford, England jail for preaching salvation by grace through faith, which was contrary to the doctrine of the established church in England. The story is told that on one occasion he was offered his freedom, if he would promise not to preach this again. He steadfastly refused to make such a pledge and remained in jail until the law was relaxed.

Strangely, those who left Europe in order to escape religious persecution soon began to leave America for the same reason. And again Baptists were the chief sufferers. However, they continued to present a united front in the cause of religious liberty. Because of his religious views, in the dead of the winter of 1636 Roger Williams was banished from the Massachusetts Bay Colony. Except for friendly Indians he might well have died. Two years later he founded Providence, Rhode Island. Thus for the first time in more than thirteen hundred years, since Constantine adopted Christianity, there existed a political body where church and state were separated. Of course, this meant a guarantee of religious liberty. It marked a new beginning of a new era in the world's spiritual career.

Though Williams was not a Baptist at the time, he became one in 1639. None of his small group had been baptized after a profession of faith. Williams was baptized by Earl Holliman. In turn he baptized Holliman and eleven others. Later, troubled because of his irregular manner of being baptized, Williams left the church there to become a ''seeker.''

Who can forget the 1651 account of the public whipping in Boston of Obadiah Holmes for participating in an unauthorized worship service in the home of an aged and blind Baptist in Lynn, Massachusetts? Or Henry Dunster, the first president of Harvard University, forced to resign and banished from the colony for refusing to have his child baptized in infancy?

In Virginia the battle for a free church was long and hard. The struggle involved freedom of worship and freedom from taxation to support the established church. John Leland eventually came from Massachusetts to lead in this struggle. Virginia Baptists were largely alone in this effort so far as religious bodies were concerned. However, though not Baptists, some statesmen (James Madison, Thomas Jefferson, and George Washington) championed their cause.

The Presbyterians opposed the established church (Episcopal). A bill was introduced in the Virginia General Assembly in 1784 which provided for a tax to support teachers of religion, each person being allowed to designate which religious teacher his assessment would support. In one of his letters James Madison wrote: "The Episcopal clergy are generally for it . . . . The Presbyterians seem as ready to set up an establishment which would take them in as they were to pull one down which shut them out. The Baptists, however, standing firmly by their avowed principle of the complete separation of church and state, declared it to be 'repugnant to the spirit of the Gospel for the Legislature thus to proceed in matters of religion that no human laws ought to be established for the purpose.' " [6] (It should be noted that the Methodists were a newly formed group whose influence was scarcely felt in such matters. According to the record, as a body they took no part in this struggle.)

When the Federal Constitution was written the Baptists of Virginia insisted that it contained no guarantee of religious liberty. James Madison was a candidate in his county for a seat in that state's ratifying convention. There is a question as to whether John Leland was also a candidate. A manuscript by Eugene Bucklin Bowen of Cheshire, Massachusetts, now in the Library of Congress, says that Leland was a candidate. The Madison Papers, also in the Library of Congress, mention a Colonel Barbour as a candidate. Since there were several candidates, both statements could be true. Regardless, Leland was the one man to be dealt with.[7] So Madison and Leland met under an oak tree near Orange.

After a long and hot discussion it was agreed that the Baptist candidate would withdraw (whether Leland or a Colonel Barbour) on condition that Madison would join Leland in a crusade for an amendment to the Constitution guaranteeing religious liberty, free speech, and a free press. Madison won the election. But no such amendment was made. Since the Baptists continued to regard Madison highly, it may be assumed that he made an honest effort in this regard but without success. (His one great fear, expressed to Leland in the oak tree conference, was that if such an item was included in the Constitution, Massachusetts and some other states would not ratify it.)

In 1789 Leland was commissioned by the Baptists to write to President George Washington about the lack of a guarantee of religious liberty. Washington replied to assure that such a guarantee should be provided.[8] Through James Madison the first amendment to the Constitution was presented and adopted. It reads in part, "Congress shall make no law respecting an establishment of religion, or prohibiting the free exercise thereof." This wholly satisfied the Baptists, who promptly expressed that satisfaction to Madison.

Dawson comments: "If the researchers of the world were asked who was most responsible for the American guarantee for religious liberty, their prompt reply would be 'James Madison'; but if James Madison might answer, he would as quickly reply, 'John Leland and the Baptists.' "[9]

Soul Freedom a Baptist Principle

There is no evidence that Baptists came to their view of soul freedom and separation of church and state gradually. Nowhere in their history is there a wavering note on this great theme. It seems to have been a divinely given prophetic insight into the meaning of the gospel and the implicit teaching of Scripture. Note *implicit teaching*. For Scripture nowhere enjoins in so many words separation of church and state. Perhaps the nearest thing to it is Jesus' statement about rendering to both Caesar and God the things pertaining to them (Matt. 22:21). However, even here it is a derived meaning, not a verbatim teaching as such. It required spiritual discernment and prophetic insight of a high order to discover the doctrine; and yet when once discovered by the unbiased mind, it was accepted as a self-evident truth.

This is all the more amazing when we recall the struggle for supremacy between church and state from the time of Constantine to that of

Pope Gregory VII. In the latter the spirit of the Roman Church became incarnate. The complete triumph of the church over the state is seen in Gregory's act in releasing the subjects of Emperor Henry from allegiance to him. To regain it he was required to do penance by standing barefoot in the snow at Canossa. The church's victory is evident also in Gregory's letter to William the Conqueror to the effect that the state was subordinate to the church, that the power of the state as compared to that of the church was as the moon compared to the sun.

The great Reformers Martin Luther and John Calvin did not rise to the conception of the separation of church and state; they even used civil power to enforce religion. It was the persecuted Anabaptists who sounded this note in that period. In doing so many of them paid with their lives. Even today in Great Britain this unnatural alliance of church and state continues.

In the American colonies apart from Rhode Island and Virginia, where Baptists led the way, the nearest approach to the true ideal was one form or another of religious toleration. In no American colony save in the two mentioned was there even an effort made to establish religious liberty in the true sense. The Calverts in Maryland secured a charter from England which granted a certain amount of toleration. To these Roman Catholics this move seemed like a great stride forward. In comparison with their usual insistence upon an ironclad Church authority and their exclusive claim to apostolicity, it was a real step in advance. But the Baptists stood for a more thoroughgoing principle than Romanist or Protestant in their doctrine of complete separation of church and state. Toleration and religious liberty are poles apart.

In America, even where in some cases religious toleration existed, Baptists still contended for religious liberty. Worthy of note is the fact that even the Declaration of Independence failed to include religious oppression among the tyrannies that should be eliminated. It was as Madison, Adams, and others said—the idea of a free church in a free state was foreign to the general philosophy and social theories of the age. Men imagined that to adopt the principle would be to open the floodgates to infidelity in a thousand forms. But Baptists continued to stand for this principle.

Historical Significance of Baptists

We are now ready to deal with the claim of Baptists to their unique historical significance. What great principle have they contributed to the religious life and thought of mankind? Or what interpretation of Christianity do they represent that distinguishes them from all other Christian bodies?

In answering these questions we will find that there are a number of great elementary truths, of the nature of axioms, which lie at the heart of the Baptist conception of Christianity. These universal and self-evident truths are simply the expression of the universal elements in Christianity and thus serve as the best statement of what the religion of Christ is in its essential nature. What then is the distinguishing Baptist principle?

Immediately we recognize certain great principles which have been consistently and are now readily identified with Baptists. One is the *separation of church and state*. However, it is possible for Baptists to have this, yet for Roman Catholicism to remain as the form of Christianity that survives. Doctrinally this system is at the opposite pole from Baptists. If such should be the case, it would simply mean spiritual tyranny, even though the church would remain free from civil control. Soul freedom is not the end but the means. The goal is self-realization through Christ. Freedom by itself does not imply capacity for self-government, and any adequate statement of the New Testament teaching must include this. Another position is *individualism in spiritual matters*. But this is inadequate. For man is more than an individual; he is a social being. He has relations to his fellows in other areas of life: church, economic order, and state. Again, there is the basic message of *salvation by grace through faith*. This, however, is shared with certain other Christian groups. So it cannot be called distinctively Baptist in nature. As precious as are other doctrines (lordship of Christ, regenerated church membership, democracy, and the priesthood of the believers), no one of these can be identified only with Baptists. All of these are vitally important and grow directly out of Baptists' fundamental position. But they are corollaries to a prior truth. They are not original but derived.

The statement of the historical significance of Baptists in this: *the competency of the soul in religion.* Of course, this means a competency under God, not a competency of human self-sufficiency. There is no reference here to the question of sin and human ability in the moral and theological sense, nor in the sense of independence of the Scriptures. This is not a creed; Baptists are not a creedal people. To the contrary, it stands as a safeguard against coercion with respect to solidifying one's faith in the form of a written creed. This should not be interpreted to mean that a person can believe anything he chooses and call himself a Baptist. Baptists are identified with truth as taught in the Scriptures, the criterion for the interpretation of which is Jesus Christ. But this competency stands as a flaming sword to protect the individual conscience in matters of faith and its relation to God.

The Baptist position at this point was expressed many years ago by George W. Truett. In effect he said that a true Baptist will not use the pressure of his little finger to force someone to become a Baptist against his will. But he will rise from his bed at midnight to protect one's right not to be a Baptist against his will. Such is a matter between him and God, not between him and another man.

This conception of the competency of the soul under God in religion is both exclusive and inclusive in a measure that sets forth the distinctive contribution of Baptists to the religious thought of the race. It is, of course, a New Testament principle of one's relations to God which was taught by Jesus Christ himself.

The competency of the soul in religion excludes all human interference such as episcopacy, infant baptism, and religion by proxy. Religion is a personal matter between the soul and God. But it is also inclusive in nature. It includes salvation by grace through faith or justification by faith. This asserts that man is competent to deal directly with God. It naturally follows that it calls for a regenerated church membership. But it also goes beyond the individualism of regeneration to the social aspect in which redeemed individuals work cooperatively, not only in worship and evangelism but in meeting the social and spiritual needs of the social order. Furthermore, soul competency calls for the separation of church and state. Since man's spiritual dealings are directly with God in Christ, there is no role for the state to play in supplying what it deems to be lacking in soul competency. State churches stand on the assumption that civil government is necessary as a factor in man's life in order to fulfill his religious destiny, that without the aid of the state man is not competent in religion.

Also there is no conceivable reason why religious authority should be vested in an infallible church, pope, or bench of bishops. This fact naturally calls for the priesthood of believers and leads naturally to democracy in local church government and in other segments of denominational structure. The competency of the regenerated individual is derived from the indwelling Christ through his Holy Spirit. Man's capacity in self-government in religion is nothing more or less than the authority of Christ exerted in and through the inner life of the believer—with the understanding always, of course, that he regulates that inner life in accordance with his revealed Word. There is, therefore, no conceivable justification for placing ecclesiastical authority in the hands of an infallible pope or a bench of bishops.

Democracy in church government is an inevitable corollary of the general doctrine of the soul's competency in religion. The independence and autonomy of the local church, therefore, is not merely an inference from a proof text here and there. It inheres in the whole philosophy of Christianity. Democracy in church government is simply Christ himself animating his own body through his Spirit. The decisions of the local congregation on ecclesiastical matters are the "consensus of the competent."

The priesthood of all believers, again, is but the expression of the soul's competency on the Godward side, as democracy is in its expression on the ecclesiastical side of its religious life. No human priest may claim to be mediator between the soul and God. The principle of competency itself meets the Roman Catholic plea against direct individual obedience to the Scriptures on the ground of the man's incapacity to interpret Scripture for himself. The right of private judgment as to the meaning of the Bible is, of course, another aspect of the same great truth.

Several things, therefore, may be said in summarizing the claim that the soul's competency in religion under God is the *historical* significance of the Baptists. (1) The biblical significance of the Baptists is the right of private interpretation of and obedience to the Scriptures. (2) The significance of the Baptists in relation to the individual is soul freedom. (3) The ecclesiastical significance of the Baptists is a regenerated church membership and the equality and priesthood of believers. (4) The political significance of the Baptists is the separation of church and state. All of these grow out of the doctrine of the soul's competency in religion under God.

Underlying the principle of soul competency are four great truths. (1) Man is made in God's image. Thus he is a person with the capacity of choice. He is free to choose—to say yes or no, even to God. But he is responsible for his choices. (2) God is able to reveal himself to man. (3) Man has a capacity for God. (4) God can and does communicate with man. These truths underlie the entire Christian movement. The incarnation of God in Christ is the one great historic expression of it.

Authenticating the Claim

If we are to claim soul competency in religion as the distinctive contribution of the Baptists to the religious thought of mankind, we should be prepared to prove it. This must be done by comparing the Baptist position with those of other religious groups within Christendom.

When this truth is laid alongside Roman Catholicism, it is quite evident that their system is the direct antithesis of the doctrine of the soul's competency. It asserts on every hand the soul's incompetency in religion. For in its system the human spirit is dependent in religion upon other human spirits. This denies the soul's competency to deal with God directly for and within itself.

Actually this is the practical result of the Roman hierarchical system as opposed to the democratic process found in the New Testament. In the Roman system the laity are dependent upon the priesthood. Within the system itself each lower order of the priesthood is dependent upon the next above it—which ultimately means that the seat of authority is in the papacy.

The order of the sacraments also denies the competency of the soul in religion. Baptism and the Lord's Supper (Mass) are valid only when, except in certain emergencies, they are administered by priestly hands. Outside the church there is no salvation. Christ and the soul alone are not equal to the redemptive task. (In an effort to evade this awkward position in modern times, the Vatican Council declared that some people not openly identified with the Roman church are actually a part of it.) In the Mass the Lord's Supper is nothing until the elements are changed by the priestly touch into the body and blood of Christ. Communion with Christ is thus removed from the realm of the Spirit and transferred to the realm of matter. And the material elements necessary to the communion are held in the form of an ecclesiastical monopoly by a human priesthood.

Auricular confession also assumes that in prayer man is incompetent to deal directly with God. A human priest must pronounce absolution. The penance, which the priest also imposes, raises a barrier between a broken heart and the forgiving Father in heaven. It asserts that his pardoning love, instead of rolling in like a tide upon the penitent soul, expands and contracts in accordance with the severity or leniency of an erring human mediator.

Again, Christ cannot call a man into his ministry; and no man can respond to that call outside the line of apostolic succession. The sacrament of orders limits Christ's ministry to an ecclesiastical chain which at no point must be broken and which at once pronounces the decree of condemnation upon all others and asserts that the alleged direct call into the ministry from Christ himself is a delusion.

Extreme unction says that God's grace in the heart cannot fit a man for the exodus through death out of this life into the next. One's dying in Christ is dependent upon a priestly mediation. Even in death the fetters of bondage to a human priesthood are not broken. For even then the gates of purgatory open only through priestly intercession on earth.

Soul incompetency is inherent in the doctrine of papal infallibility. This plus an authoritative tradition forbids all private or divergent interpretations of Scripture. For the Catholic to discover and proclaim an interpretation of God's Word that contradicts anything bearing the stamp of traditional or papal approval is for him to invoke upon his head the anathema of the church. Although some dissatisfaction with this view has surfaced, there do not appear to be any sweeping alterations of the historical Catholic position.

Turning from Roman Catholicism to Protestantism, we find, of course, important modifications. However, all such bodies that adhere to infant baptism and/or episcopacy in any form come short of the New Testament principle of the competency of the soul in religion. Indeed, they present a dualistic Christianity. They endeavor to combine the Roman Catholic principle of incompetency with the antithetic principle of competency. Holding to justification by faith, they recognize the principle of competency; but in retaining infant baptism or episcopacy they introduce the opposite view. With respect to infant baptism, this rite deprives the child of its privilege of individual initiative in salvation and lodges in the hands of parents or sponsors the impossible task of performing an act of religious obedience of another. Such a practice is an attempt to harmonize two principles which are in direct contradiction to each other.

It should be noted that even those who administer baptism by immersion for youth and adults who have made a conscious decision for Christ, but hold to a sacramentarian view of baptism, violate soul competency in that they make salvation contingent upon what another human being does to or for them. The same may be said of the Lord's Supper if it be regarded as bestowing grace not available otherwise. Since there are so many Protestant bodies, it is impossible in the scope of this work to cover all of them in detail. Suffice it to say that if none of the above or similar conditions obtain, to that extent such a body holds to soul competency—regardless of how it may interpret other New Testament truth.

In contrast to both Catholicism and Protestantism, the principle of the competency of the soul in religion is seen in its fullness in both Baptist polity and general view of Christianity. They have consistently applied this principle at every point. Their aim is to restore original Christianity in its completeness to the human race.

Following one of his crusades in London a news reporter asked Billy

Graham to comment upon an English cleric's remark that his crusade had set Christianity back two hundred years in England. He replied that he regretted to hear that, for his purpose had been to set Christianity in England back two thousand years.

The Axioms of Religion

We are now ready to consider the Baptist faith in terms of certain universal and self-evident truths or *axioms* in religious thought. In order to make clear the Baptist position, it has been necessary to treat other matters before setting forth these axioms. And before I state them, a further word is desirable to remove certain misunderstandings concerning Baptists.

For many people the very name *Baptist* focuses their mind upon the meaning and mode of baptism. It is a short step from this to the other New Testament ordinance of the Lord's Supper or communion. There was a time when heated debates were carried on, either in personal confrontation or in print, on these two matters and upon church polity, as if they were the three basic tenets of our faith and the focal point of differences between us and other denominations. It can be said at this point that New Testament scholarship, if not the popular mind, has generally agreed that the New Testament teaches exactly what the Baptists hold on these points—especially as to the ordinances. Many denominations practice what they regard as baptism but for the most part do not teach believer's baptism. Baptists are usually called *closed communionists*. But all Christian bodies (including Roman Catholics) which observe the ordinances hold that only the *baptized* are eligible for partaking of communion. The difference, then, is not the Lord's Supper but baptism. If Baptists are *closed* anything they are *closed baptismists*.

Purely out of misunderstanding, Baptists have been termed the narrowest of the larger denominations in their doctrinal position. In fact, they are the broadest in their contention that every person is free before God, but responsible to him, with regard to his faith or lack of it.

The axioms to be treated in the remainder of this book do not spell out in detail every belief of the Baptists—for example, as to the Bible, Christ, the church, and ordinances. But they do cover in broad fashion the roots of these beliefs. They are outgrowths of the principle of soul competency in religion. They assume that the Bible is God's Word, the written record of his revelation of himself to men. Roman Catholics as a body will not agree with all of these axioms, since most of them run contrary to their hierarchical system and traditions. But if no denominational label is attached to them, it may be safely predicted that most evangelicals, even unbelievers who accept the existence of God to whom they are responsible, will accept them as basic truth regardless of what their practice may be. Indeed, since they are self-evident and universal truths, no one denomination can lay claim to them as its sole property.

These axioms of religion may be stated as follows.

1. *The theological axiom:* The holy and loving God has the right to be sovereign.
2. *The religious axiom:* All souls have an equal right to direct access to God.
3. *The ecclesiastical axiom:* All believers have a right to equal privileges in the church.
4. *The moral axiom:* To be responsible man must be free.
5. *The religio-civic axiom:* A free church in a free state.
6. *The social axiom:* Love your neighbor as yourself.

In concluding this chapter we remark that the concept of the competency of the soul in religion under God, along with the axioms of religion, expresses the truths and ideals that lie at the heart of all man's higher strivings today. These truths are so obvious when once understood, so inspiring, so self-evident, that the hungering spirit of man seizes upon them as upon the pearl of great price. They shine in their own light.

Notes

[1] William Lumpkin, *Baptist Confessions of Faith* (Philadelphia: Judson Press, 1959), p. 124.

[2] Ibid., p. 140.

[3] Ibid., p. 170.

[4] Ibid., p. 232.

[5] Ibid., p. 233.

[6] Quoted by Joseph M. Dawson, *Baptists and the American Republic* (Nashville: Broadman Press, 1956), pp. 106–107.

[7] Ibid., pp. 108–109.

[8] Ibid., pp. 116–117.

[9] Ibid., p. 117.

4 / The Theological Axiom

The Holy and Loving God Has the Right
to be Sovereign

In considering the axioms of religion the natural place to begin is with God. This is where the Bible begins: "In the beginning God created the heaven and the earth" (Gen. 1:1). This is where the Gospel begins: "In the beginning was the Word, and the Word was with God, and the Word was God" (John 1:1). Thus in both creation and redemption, "In the beginning God."

This axiom states that the holy and loving God has the right to be sovereign. With reference to God *sovereign* means that without the counsel or consent of anyone outside himself, God acts in accord with his nature and will to accomplish his benevolent and redemptive purpose. This simple definition elevates God's sovereignty above capricious tyranny to the level of loving design and purpose. Rather than repelling us in fear, it draws us to him in love. The Christian does not cower before God in fear. Rather, he comes to him in love as a child to his benevolent father (Rom. 5:15). For in his sovereignty we see God's creation of his "good" universe, his providential care for all of his creation, and his purpose of redemption of both the natural order and mankind (Gen. 1:1–31; Matt. 5:45; Rom. 8:19–25).

So the matter before us is not whether God is sovereign, but that because of his holy and loving nature he has the *right* to be sovereign. For such sovereignty involves not tyranny but benevolent rule.

Character the Basis of Sovereignty

Some people stumble over the doctrine of God's sovereignty largely because they do not understand it. They interpret it in terms of a *sovereign* earthly ruler who expresses his power in cruel selfishness. Thus they see God as merely a predestinating omnipotence, as capricious lightning or a meteor God moving across the heavens of man's hope in a lawless manner, smiting one and saving another with no regard to moral law. They think of him only as sovereign omnipotence or as sovereign omniscience instead of sovereign Fatherhood, as he is. God is fatherly in his nature. He longs to be the Father of all people. But he is Father in truth only to those who have become his children through faith in his essential, eternal Son (John 1:12). If God is holy and loving, if he has moral character, he has the right to be sovereign. And the Bible presents him as such.

God is *holy*. In Leviticus 19:2 Jehovah said, "I the Lord [*Yahweh*, Jehovah, specific name for Israel's God] your God [*Elohim*, general name for God] am holy" (see Lev. 21:8). In his prayer in John 17 Jesus addressed God as "Holy Father" (v. 11). In both Isaiah 6:3 and Revelation 4:8 the heavenly hosts praise him as thrice "Holy." Furthermore, things and people related to him are described as "holy" (Ex. 30:25–37; Lev. 8:9; 16:2–4; 21:7; 27:30). Israel was to be a "holy nation" (Ex. 19:6; 1 Pet. 2:9).

Basically both the Hebrew and Greek words for "holy" mean separation, set apart, or dedicated. In pagan religions they carried no moral sense. Women used in the worship of sex deities were called holy women. It was when the words for *holy* came to be used of God that they took on the moral sense of his nature. Thus God is not adorned by the word *holy*. Rather, because of his character he elevated the word to its highest meaning. God's holiness is in this sense the equivalent of his *righteousness*. Thus we can ask with assurance Abraham's question, "Shall not the Judge of all the earth do right?" (Gen. 18:25). And with the psalmist in a Hebrew parallelism we can declare, "The Lord is righteous in all his ways, and holy in all his works" (Ps. 145:17).

The holiness of God depicts his righteous character. But it also expresses his transcendence. He created the universe and abides in it, but he is not contained by it. He is not limited by either time or space. He transcends all, is over all, and yet is nearer to us than breath itself. Nevertheless, his nearness should not produce an attitude of overfamiliarity on our part. He is not simply "the man upstairs" but the God of the universe. As to Moses he says to us, "Draw not nigh hither: put off thy shoes from off thy feet, for the place whereon thou standest is holy ground'' (Ex. 3:5).

Furthermore, God is *loving*. First John 4:8 declares that ''God is love.'' Other than the word for sexual attraction, which does not appear in the New Testament, the Greek language had two words for love: one (*philos*) expressed the warm love of friendship; the other (*agape*) was regarded as a colder word. Thus in classical Greek the former predominates, while the latter is used sparingly. It could be that this scarcity led the Holy Spirit to choose this latter word to express the very nature of God.

In the New Testament *philos* and its kindred words are used sparingly. *Agape* and its kindred words appear 330 times. Of interest also is the fact that the word for holy (*hagios*) is used 229 times. Both families of words are used of both God or Deity and of people and places related to him. A holy, loving God should have a holy, loving people.

It is difficult to translate the word *agape* into English. The late W. Hersey Davis, professor of New Testament at Southern Baptist Theological Seminary, said in my presence that the word connotes absolute loyalty to its object. He is reported on another occasion to have said that the one English word which most nearly translates it is *selflessness*. Thus these two words speak volumes about God's holy, righteous nature and his selfless love for all people. It is God's will to do the greatest amount of good for the greatest number of people.

God's character is seen in his saving purpose. The ''little gospel'' (John 3:16) declares God's love for the world. But also the word ''perish'' involves his holy, righteous nature. [1] Since God does not will that anyone perish, he gave his only Son as Savior. Christ died not for God's friends but for his enemies—those in rebellion against him. ''God commendeth his love toward us, in that, while we were yet sinners, Christ died for us'' (Rom. 5:8). ''God was in Christ, reconciling the world unto himself'' (2 Cor. 5:19). Repeatedly the Bible calls upon men to be reconciled to God. But nowhere does it say that he needs to be reconciled to the world. Were that the case there would have been no offer of salvation. God has taken the initiative; he but waits in love for man's positive response.

Romans 1:17–18 says that in the gospel are revealed both God's *righteousness* and *wrath*. These correspond to his *love* and *holiness* respectively. In the Bible *righteousness* is used for what God is in his nature; for that which he demands in man; for that which man cannot achieve in his own power; and for that which God in Christ bestows upon him.

In Romans *righteousness* refers primarily to God's saving activity whereby he picks a lost sinner up out of the wrong and places him down in the right as though he had never been in the wrong. The Greek word (*dikaiosune*) belongs to a family of nouns ending with the letter *eta*. These words do not mean that a thing is necessarily true, but that one chooses to regard it as true. Thus one is not necessarily righteous, but in Christ God regards him as being so. This is an activity of his love and grace. And this righteousness comes to a person by God's grace through faith in his Son. In Romans 4 Paul showed that even Abraham was saved not by works such as circumcision and keeping the law, but by faith. Using a bookkeeping term, he said that when Abraham believed God, it was put down to his account as righteousness (Gen. 15:6).

Wrath, on the other hand, is not an emotion of God but his law in operation. That we might live in a cosmos instead of a chaos, God has ordained law in the natural, physical, moral, and spiritual realms. These laws are intended to provide the greatest amount of good for the greatest number of people. They are designed to be a blessing, not a blight. It is only when we live contrary to them that they take their toll. Wrath relates to the toll for breaking God's spiritual law (Rom. 6:23). It connotes God's abiding universal opposition to the evil that violates his holiness. John the Baptist used this word in Matthew 3:7. The picture is that of snakes fleeing before a desert or prairie fire. Since it is everywhere, where can one flee from it? The only place of safety is where the fire has already burned. The only safe place from God's wrath is at Calvary, where in love for a lost humanity he poured out his wrath upon his Son. This he did in love for lost people as he satisfied the demands of his holy, righteous nature whereby he might provide the basis for the forgiveness of sin for all who believe in Jesus.

Once men recognize God's character behind his sovereignty, they have little or no problem in accepting it. Indeed, as a matter of logic there is no standing ground in the intellect of man for any theory that is opposed to God's sovereignty. An aged philosopher was asked what, if he had just one question to ask, it would be. He replied, "Is the universe friendly?" To find the answer he has only to look at Calvary. It is thus that the holy and loving God has the right to be sovereign. And no one needs to fear to come under his sovereign will.

God's Sovereignty in Nature

In years past a purely materialistic philosophy and science tended to deny God's sovereignty—in many quarters, even his existence. They stressed the eternity of matter and the helplessness of man in the order of nature. He was regarded as an atom played upon by irresistible forces of blind chance. Even Deism, while admitting the possibility of a Person back of the natural order, looked upon an absentee God who created the universe, wound it up, and left it to run for itself. This also left man as a helpless victim of impersonal forces beyond his or any other person's control.

Science is no longer so dogmatic in its view of a purely materialistic universe. Today many of those out on the frontier of scientific advance see behind and within the natural order a Person—by whatever name they may call him. The late Arthur Compton, a physicist of the highest order, was quoted in a Chicago newspaper to the effect that "in the beginning God" are the noblest words ever penned. Sir James Jeans, an English mathematician, said that back of the universe is a great "mathematical Mind." Of interest is the fact that when man split the atom, the building block of the universe, he did not use a hammer and chisel but a mathematical equation.

Who can ever forget the worldwide thrill when, on Christmas Eve several years ago, astronauts circling the moon read the creation story from Genesis 1? Astronaut Ronald Evans, commander of the *Apollo 17* mission, said that viewing planet Earth from a distance made it clear that "it's too beautiful and perfect for it to have happened by accident, that there is someone greater than us all."

This view corresponds to the Bible account of creation. Time itself, as well as matter, stems from "In the beginning God created the heaven and the earth" (Gen. 1:1). In Isaiah 45:12 Jehovah said, "I have made the earth, and created man upon it: I, even my hands, have stretched out the heavens, and all their hosts [heavenly bodies] have I commanded."

While the Bible mentions the three Persons of the Godhead in relation to creation, its emphasis is upon Christ as the intermediate agent in the creative work. So the Redeemer is also the Creator. Literally, John 1:3 reads, "Every single thing in the universe through him came into being; and apart from him there came into being not even one thing which has come into being." In the same vein Paul in Colossians 1:15 said that Christ is "the firstborn of every creature." The word for "firstborn" means just that in Luke 2:7. But to see this meaning in Colossians makes Christ a created being, the very thing Paul would not imply. This word is also used in the sense of prior existence with the resultant meaning of "lord." [2] So, literally, Paul said that Christ is "Lord of every single part of creation." In verse 16 "all things" means the universe as a whole. Combining the ideas of John and Paul, Christ is the creator of the universe from atoms to multiplied solar systems.

But Paul went one step further. In Colossians 1:17 he said, literally, "And he himself is before the universe in its several parts, and the universe as a whole in him stands together" or "holds together." What men once thought was the universe we now know to be but one solar system among what one astronomer estimates to be fourteen quadrillion of such, each with its own sun and billions of stars. No longer can we speak of a geocentric or heliocentric universe. If neither the earth nor the sun is the center of the universe, who or what is? Almost two thousand years ago, writing under the inspiration of the Holy Spirit, Paul told us. We live in a Christ-centered or Christocentric universe! Not a sun-centered but a Son-centered universe.

That God is sovereign in the natural universe is seen in the precision with which it moves. Astronomers can tell us where a given star will be in the heavens one thousand years from now, if the Lord delays his return.

We see God's sovereignty in the law of gravity, by which everything on earth is held in place. We see it even more clearly in the laws of the seasons. Thus farmers know when to sow and when to expect a harvest. Life on earth depends not upon the accidents of blind chance in the natural order, but upon the constancy of the laws of a holy, loving God. Even the atmosphere is of a proper constituency to make possible life on earth. Ecologists are concerned that man's machinations may disturb this constituency. God made the earth *good*, and everything wrong with it is man's doing as he disregards the laws of God.

We are told that the earth is at the exact angle on its axis for life to exist on earth. Should it shift one degree either way the earth would become either a charred cinder or an iceberg. Surely the astronaut was correct when, while hurtling back toward earth from a barren moon, he said, "God did something special on earth!"

Now the natural laws of God do not mean that he is a prisoner in his own universe. Thus there is no reason to doubt his power to work miracles. A miracle is an act of God—contrary to natural law as man understands it, but not contrary to law as God understands it—which he performs in keeping with his benevolent will and purpose. Today we take for granted such things as airplanes and television—which a few years ago would have been regarded as miracles. By the law of aerodynamics man is able to rise above the law of gravity. While man has known of this law only since the Wright brothers, it has been in God's infinite mind from eternity. Who can say what laws are still known to God which man has yet to discover—or, better still, have revealed to him?

If one truly accepts the first four words of the Bible, "In the beginning God," he will have no trouble accepting the rest of it: for example, Jesus' virgin birth, miracles, atoning death, bodily resurrection, and all the rest. Man must not seek to limit the infinite God by his finite being! Rather, we must see him as the holy, loving, benevolent, and infinite God working in his universe in a manner in keeping with his nature and purpose.

One question ever confronts us. If God can make a cosmos out of his universe, is he not able to make one out of our chaotic world and lives? Thus God is sovereign in nature not only by right of his creative work, but by right of his providential care. The universe is a cosmos, not a chaos. Its cosmic character speaks to the character of its Creator who created it with loving design and purpose (Rom. 1:20). He showers his love upon all people regardless of their own spiritual nature (Matt. 5:45). But his loving acts are expressions of his saving will in that even for the unbelieving they are designed to bring man to repentance (Rom. 2:4; Jas. 1:17).

God's Sovereignty in History

Thus God's holy and loving sovereignty is evident in the affairs of men and nations. This fact throws light upon perplexing problems in both history and nature. This does not mean that God is responsible for the evil doings of men and nations. His foreknowledge of events is in keeping with his attributes of omnipresence and omniscience. But foreknowledge of events does not necessarily mean that God causes them. At the finite level you may know that two cars are going to collide at an intersection. But this does not mean that you cause it. Because of his omnipresence God knows all things simultaneously, without need of reason or thought processes. But it is contrary to the Bible's presentation of God's nature as holy, righteous, and loving to attribute to him the evil that transpires in the world.

However one may explain the origin of evil, he cannot be true to biblical truth or practical experience in making God its originating cause. For one thing we must take into account man's freedom of choice, a subject to be discussed later. We must recognize God's benevolent laws; defiance of them brings disaster. And we must accept the Bible's recognition of Satan, whose evil purpose is to thwart God's benevolent purposes in both man and nature.

Take, for example, the lesson of the book of Job. It is designed to refute the popular idea, ancient and modern, that a given suffering is the direct result of a given sin—that a vengeful God hurls his thunderbolts of wrath upon those who defy his will. When tragedy strikes it is so easy to ask, Is this God's will? Job 1—2 answers this question with a resounding *no!*

Satan slandered Job to God, saying that the patriarch served God out of only selfish motives. Then he challenged God to afflict Job and see how quickly he would turn on God. God refused, but he permitted Satan to do it. Out of love he gave Job the opportunity to refute Satan's slander. And every evil thing which befell him—robbery, murder, natural disasters, and Job's illness—was Satan's work. Job's famous words "The Lord gave, and the Lord hath taken away" (Job 1:21) are but half right. From his limited perspective they were right. But to the viewer of the entire tragic drama it is clear that the Lord gave, but Satan took away.

It should be noted, however, that in his holy and loving sovereignty God kept Satan on a leash (Job 1:21; 2:6). He permitted the evil one to go so far but no farther. So that even in the evil which befalls us, we can find grounds for thanksgiving. Samuel Rutherford once said, "My faith has no bed to sleep upon but omnipotency." This truth is enhanced beyond measure when we recall that it is a holy, loving omnipotency.

Actually, in Job we see three facets of God's will. His *intentional* will was to do only good for Job. In the dire circumstance his *circumstantial* will was that Job trust him through it. His *ultimate* will was that his intentional will ultimately would be done, as seen in Job's greater blessings after the ordeal (Job 42:12–17).

A holy and loving God *permits* some things that he does not *perpe-trate*. He does not seal away his children in sterilized plastic bags to protect them from the harsh realities of life; else Satan's charge would be true. God is not in the business of growing hothouse plants, but virile timber which grows in character as it endures the blasts of many storms. Thus he wills that in the adverse circumstances of life we will trust him, find strength in him, and grow into his likeness in the process.

In such experiences Paul found God's grace sufficient. "Therefore I take pleasure in infirmities, in reproaches, in necessities, in persecutions, in distresses for Christ's sake: for when I am weak, then am I strong" (2 Cor. 12:10). Jesus said, "In the world ye shall have tribulation; but be of good cheer [courage]; I have overcome [fully conquered] the world" (John 16:33).

As the storm of the crucifixion was about to break upon his disciples, Jesus said, "Let not your heart be troubled: ye believe in God, believe also in me" (John 14:1). "Be troubled" expresses the idea of an ocean caught in the teeth of a storm. In their *storm* Jesus prescribed faith in God and his Son as the secret of an untroubled heart.

Revelation 4—5 was written within the context of persecution. Looking *about* at earthly events, Christians thought that all was lost. But God told John to look *up* and see what was transpiring in heaven! John saw "a throne was set in heaven, and one sat on the throne" (4:2). And that one was not the emperor Domitian, but God. "Was set" means that there was never a time when this was not true. God was being praised for his creative work. John saw redeemed saints and a redeemed nature also praising the Lamb for his redemptive work (Rev. 5). The sense is that history can be understood only in light of God's redemptive purpose in Christ. One has noted that in chapter 4 the Lord is saying, "Believe in God." In chapter 5 he is saying, "Believe also in me." [3]

Thus God is sovereign in the broader history of mankind. Historiographers may record the migration of a band of once-enslaved Israelites from Egypt to Canaan. But *holy history,* or history within history, sees God working amid the tragedy of history to prepare a people and to locate them in a strategic base at the crossroads of the ancient world, whereby they might be used as a priest-nation to bring pagan nations to worship him (Ex. 19:1–8). Likewise, historiographers relate the conquests of Alexander the Great and of Rome. But holy history points to the fact that, despite man's cruelty, a holy, loving God worked to provide an almost universal language (*Koine* Greek) and to establish roads and sea lanes whereby his evangels of grace might go from Jerusalem to the ends of the Roman world to preach his gospel of salvation to all who believe in Jesus. In his holy history, salvation history, despite the struggle and trouble of human history, eyes of faith see God in the shadows and, in his own time and way, distilling from evil brew the pure honey of his redemptive will and purpose.

A skeptic asked why, if God proposed to redeem the world through Jesus Christ, did he have him to be born, to live, and to die in a practically unknown and despised land on the backside of the world? In so asking he only displayed his ignorance of ancient history. For Palestine, small though it was, formed a land bridge between desert and sea over which the traffic of the ancient world moved to and from

Africa, Asia, and Europe, the three known continents of that era. So God's redemptive purpose was wrought out in *the center of the world!* And from there the bearers of the gospel were sent to Jerusalem, Judea, Samaria, and the uttermost parts of the earth (Acts 1:8). This is but one example of how the limited intelligence of man seeks to challenge the infinite mind of God.

Romans 8:28 is often quoted as a favorite verse of Scripture. But unfortunately the King James Version does not clearly express the meaning. The verb for "work together" is third person singular. Therefore, "all things" (plural) cannot be the subject. Literally it reads: "We know perceptively that to the ones loving God, with respect to every single thing he [God] works together unto good, to the ones being called according to his purpose." Paul defined this purpose in Ephesians 2:15: "That he might create in himself one new man in place of two, so making peace" (RSV). This is the equation of life. One Jew plus one Gentile plus Christ equals two Christian brethren. Use any combination of classes, nationalities, or races, and the answer is the same.

Earlier in Ephesians (1:9–10) the apostle went one step further. "Having made known unto us the mystery of his will, according to his good pleasure which he hath purposed in himself: that in the dispensation of the fulness of times he might gather together in one all things [the universe as a whole, both natural and spiritual] in Christ." "Gather together" raises a mental picture of an army scattered in battle being brought together again and formed into a fighting force. Both man and the natural order have been scattered by evil. In Christ God is regrouping this scattered force.

When man sinned he became out of fellowship with God. In a way unknown to us the natural order also *fell*. And according to Romans 8:19–22 in a way unknown to us Christ also is redeeming the natural order along with a lost humanity.

Yes, as Benjamin Franklin once said, "God governs in the affairs of men; and if a sparrow cannot fall to the ground without His notice, it is improbable that an empire can rise without his aid." This is in keeping with Paul's words spoken on Mars' Hill in Athens. God "hath determined the times before appointed, and the bounds of their habitation"

(Acts 17:26). No nation emerges from the womb of time apart from God's will. And no nation sinks into the grave of eternity without his notice. The heathen may rage and imagine vain things, but "he that sitteth in the heavens shall laugh: the Lord shall have them in derision" (Ps. 2:4).

God's Sovereignty and the Incarnation

God's sovereignty expressed in terms of holiness and love is the heart of the gospel. The incarnation of God in Christ is the greatest of all conceivable expressions of that sovereignty. It is an expression of a sovereignty of power, to be sure; but most of all it is an expression of the sovereignty of character, the sovereignty of holy and loving Fatherhood. God gave his Son, and the Son fully revealed his Father. Thus God manifested his sovereignty by taking the initiative in salvation. Such an act was not an afterthought with God. It is the index of all his sovereignty.

In a later chapter we will deal with human freedom. However, at this point we anticipate it by noting that any doctrine of divine sovereignty must safeguard man's freedom. Though God does not compel a lost person to be saved, God's offer of grace is so designed as to produce a compulsion within the lost sinner, as the Holy Spirit reveals God's character as holiness and love. God identified himself with man completely, apart from sin, that he might draw lost men to himself in a free and loving response. This he did in the person of his Son. Christ is the Lamb "slain from the foundation of the world" (Rev. 13:8). Thus forgiveness was in God's heart before sin was in man's heart (see Heb. 10:5–7).

When God revealed his law he did so through a man, Moses. When he revealed his grace he *became* a man, Jesus of Nazareth (John 1:14).

The earliest point of beginning in the Gospels is in John 1:1— literally, "In the beginning always was the Word [Christ], and the Word always was equal with God, and the Word always was God himself." Thus in one terse sentence John declared the coeternity, coequality, and coexistence of Christ with the Father. Then he moved from eternity into time in saying, "And the Word was made [became] flesh, and dwelt [tabernacled] among us (and we beheld his glory, the glory as of the only begotten of the Father), full of grace and truth" (John 1:14). Note the change of the verb from "was" (v. 1) to "became" (v. 14). The former states essential being. The latter means that Christ *became* what he had not been before—a flesh-and-blood man! It is true that Jesus was God. But a far more thrilling truth is that God *became* Jesus of Nazareth—for us.

The author of Hebrews began by noting the climax of God's various revelations of himself when he spoke to men in the person of one bearing to him the relation of "Son" (1:2). In Colossians 1:15 Paul called Christ the "image [*eikōn,* icon, exact manifestation] of the invisible God." He described not a God who simply has not been seen, but one who cannot be seen by the natural eye. "God is spirit" (John 4:24, RSV). In order to be seen he became flesh so that Jesus could say, "He that hath seen me hath seen the Father" (John 14:9). Probably the greatest statement of the full deity of Jesus Christ is in Colossians 2:9, which reads literally, "Because in him alone is permanently at home every single part of the essence of deity, the state of being God, in bodily form."

Some deny that Jesus ever claimed deity. Only one citation to the contrary is necessary. "I and my Father are one" (John 10:30). For this the Jews attempted to stone him to death "for blasphemy; and because that thou, being a man, makest thyself God" (v. 33). Some modern critics may have missed the point. But these on-the-scene Jewish scholars caught it.

This grand truth implies the virgin birth as reported by both Matthew and Luke (Gal. 4:4). How else could Jesus be the Son of God? If one denies the virgin birth on the basis of the absence of specific mention of it by Mark, John, and Paul, only one question needs to be asked. *How many times does the Bible need to say something for it to be true?* As a matter of fact Mark began his Gospel with the public ministry of John the Baptist and Jesus. So there was no point in his mentioning Jesus' birth. And only a prejudiced mind can fail to see the virgin birth in John 1:14 and Galatians 4:4–5. All three writers (Mark, John, and Paul) present Jesus as the Son of God. The burden of proof lies with those who deny the virgin birth to show how Jesus could be God's Son in any other than a virgin birth.

Jesus also lived a sinless life, though tempted at all points like as we are, yet without sin (Matt. 4:1–11; Luke 4:1–13; Heb. 4:15). Someone has said that for Jesus to live in a flesh-and-blood body in a corrupt social order and be tempted at all points without sinning once is as great a miracle in the moral sphere as is a virgin birth in the physical sphere.

That brings us to the question of the why of the incarnation. Is God unjust in his demand for perfect righteousness in man? The incarnation answers in the negative. Paul stated it thus: "To declare, I say, at this time his righteousness: that he might be just, and the justifier of him which believeth in Jesus" (Rom. 3:26). In his sinless life Jesus showed God *just* in his demand. Having done so, in his death and resurrection he showed God as the *justifier* of all who believe in Jesus. The apostle stated it in another way—literally, "The one not knowing sin experientially, on our behalf he made sin, in order that we on the other hand might become God's righteousness in him" (2 Cor. 5:21; cf. Isa. 53:4–6).

The author of Hebrews said that animal sacrifice was but the shadow of the truth which was in Jesus' death (10:1). Why was not animal sacrifice sufficient? Because it involved only brute animals, unwilling sacrifices with no concept of what was involved. Christ was the one sinless, willing sacrifice with full understanding of what was involved. Man's redemption calls not for an interplay of persons with things, but of persons with the divine Person. This was accomplished in the incarnation (Phil. 2:6–11). For "God was in Christ, reconciling the world unto himself" (2 Cor. 5:19).

We do not understand the virgin birth and/or the incarnation—how in Jesus of Nazareth could be combined both deity and humanity. It is a *mystery*, something revealed by God instead of something discovered by man through reason. Take the mystery out of Christianity and you have only a philosophy. If I could understand God I could not worship him. For then my mind would be greater than God. As B. A. Copass used to say, we will simply have to be content to let God know some things we do not know. Otherwise we make our intellects our god. And intellectual idolatry is the most difficult to overcome.

Election and God's Sovereignty

No treatment of the sovereignty of God is complete without a consideration of the doctrine of election. Now God's election of men to salvation is not the arbitrary or capricious thing which some of the older and extreme forms of the doctrine of sovereignty taught—and, unhappily, some still teach. It is infinite wisdom, grace, and skill, seeking to save the world by the method which will reach the greatest number of people in the shortest time. Of course, time is no element with God. But his eternal redemptive purpose is wrought out in the arena of history. And because a sovereign God willed to save men as persons, time as we know it is involved. It is thus that we see election or choosing as a widening process.

God began with one man and one woman, created in a state of innocence but with a tendency toward sin, and placed them in the paradise of Eden. When they chose Satan's will rather than God's will, fellowship with God was ruptured. The bitter seed sown by their ill-chosen deed bore the bitter harvest of sin that brought on the flood. Thereafter, God made a new beginning in Noah. The sovereign God never changes his purpose, but he does change his people to be used in that purpose. Again, note the sad result of the world of Abraham's day.

Thus God chose a man, Abraham (Gen. 12:1–3). Afterward he chose a people, Israel (Ex. 19:1–8). Following her failure he chose his Son, the true seed of Abraham (Gal. 3:16). And from his redeeming death and resurrection flows an ever-widening stream. A sovereign God will not, cannot be defeated in his redemptive purpose. So within history as men date it God chose one man as a tiny rill in his redemptive purpose. In time it became a river of a chosen people, but a river that was practically dried up in the desert of a rejected covenant and a wasted opportunity. Yet from this frustrated river came again one man—a lonely man on a cross outside Jerusalem. And through an empty tomb the river, once frustrated, again flowed in ever-widening scope through a dedicated people empowered and led by the Holy Spirit.

The clearest presentation of election is found in Ephesians. Simply stated, the doctrine of election is two-fold: God has chosen a plan of salvation and has elected a people to propagate that plan. "Election is not to be thought of as a bare choice of so many human units by God's action independently of man's free choice and the human means employed. God elects men to respond freely. He elects men to preach persuasively and to witness convincingly. He elects to reach men through native faculties and through the church, through evangelism and education and missionary endeavor. We must include all these elements in election." [4] Whether it be in God's offer of salvation or his call to be a propagating people, we may say yes or no to him.

Against this background, let us focus upon Paul's words about election to salvation as found in Ephesians 1:4-14. "Hath chosen" (v. 4) translates the verb from which comes "election." Paul said that this election was determined "before the foundation of the world." It was made "according to the good pleasure of his will" (v. 5) or in his sovereignty.

Such a position has led many to regard God's sovereignty in election, to the neglect of man's free will. Both are evident teachings of Scripture; neither can be disregarded in considering God's dealings with men. To ignore man's free will is to see God arbitrarily electing some to salvation to the neglect of all others. In the Bible election is never presented in conflict with man's free will. God's purpose in election is to save not a few but as many as possible. Frank Stagg says, "One is strangely insensitive to the throb and pulse beat of the whole New Testament if he thinks that each man's fate is determined for him in advance. This is not a 'rigged' television show. God is not playing with toys or manipulating gadgets; he is seeking men who stand in awesome freedom where they may accept or reject the salvation which God alone can offer." [5]

The problem is much simplified when we see Paul's words as a whole. In verse 5 he told how God has elected. "In love" (v. 4, KJV) should be in verse 5. "In love having predestinated us . . . by [dia, through] Jesus Christ." However God elected, he did so in love and through Jesus Christ.

"Having predestinated" translates a verb meaning to set a boundary beforehand. It is like building a fence around a piece of land. In this case the fence is Christ. "In Christ" or its equivalent is used ten times in eleven verses (vv. 3–13). So God elected that all who are "in Christ" will be saved. All outside of Christ will be lost. He did this in holy and loving sovereignty in that he did not ask the advice or consent of anyone outside himself. Man's free will is seen in "believed" in verse 13. God's foreknowledge as to those who would or would not believe does not mean that he caused it. He offered every incentive for man to believe. The final choice lay with man. God in his sovereignty set the condition. Man in his free will determines the result. Thus there is no conflict between sovereignty and free will. Rather, they complement each other.

Verses 13–14 show how through the indwelling Holy Spirit God *seals* those who believe in Christ. This seal is evidence of God's ownership and his guarantee of safe delivery of the soul into heaven. The Spirit is also God's "earnest" or earnest money (*arrabōn*) that he will go through with the redemptive process "until" (*eis,* goal) the "full redemption" (*apolutrōsin*) of the purchased possesion. The word *arabōn* was used in the papyri for earnest money and/or a guarantee. It appears in the New Testament only here and in 2 Corinthians 1:22; 5:5. In each case it is related to the Holy Spirit. "Full redemption" involves regeneration (saving of the soul), sanctification (saving of the Christian life), and glorification (sum total of glory and reward in heaven).

God's respect for man's free will is not an evidence of his weakness but of his strength. In his sovereignty he proposes to save and use men, but within conditions of his own choosing. Man in his free will is free to accept or reject. But he is responsible to God for his choices.

God's Sovereignty Affirmed

The Scriptures picture Satan as disputing God's sovereignty in the universe. In tempting Jesus in the wilderness, he blatantly made this claim (Luke 4:6–7). God was incarnated in Jesus Christ to refute and destroy this false claim (1 John 3:8). The climax of the book of Revelation is in 11:15, where "kingdom" (singular in RSV) may read "sovereignty." Literally, "The sovereignty of the cosmos became that of our Lord [God], and of his Christ, and he shall reign as sovereign unto the ages of the ages." "Unto the ages of the ages" is the strongest Greek phrase for *eternity*.

Now when was it that this undisputed sovereignty became or came to be? It was when Jesus rose from the dead! (See "power" or "authority" in Matthew 28:18.) Evil had done its worst to God, only to fail. Much fighting remains before the end of time. But the fact of God's holy and loving sovereignty is shown without question. In the end Satan, his angels, and all with him who oppose God's sovereignty will be cast into the lake of fire (Rev. 20:10,15).

In 1 Corinthians 15:28 Paul took the farthest look into the future of any New Testament writer. He saw Christ reigning in his mediatorial kingdom, subduing the universe both natural and spiritual unto himself (vv. 25–27). "Subdue" pictures an army lined up in order under its commander (cf. Eph. 1:10). Then in verse 28 he said, literally, "And when the universe as a whole [natural and spiritual] shall be lined up as troops under him, then shall the Son also himself be lined up as a troop under him [God] lining up the entire universe under him [Christ], that God may be all in all." God the Father, Son, and Holy Spirit—but God, all in all.

Yes, a holy and loving God has the right to be sovereign. Evil men and nature may challenge his sovereignty now. But eschatological history looks to the point beyond time when that which is now a fact will be recognized in all eternity as indeed true (Phil. 2:10-11). God's intentional will ultimately will be done. A redeemed host in a redeemed universe—in the city of God—in a restored Eden (Rev. 21—22). And a holy and loving God as undisputed sovereign will dwell with his people.

Notes

[1] The verb *perish* comes from the same derivative as does *Apollyon*, the destroyer, one name for Satan (Rev. 9:11). So the passage could also be read "should not be lost in hell."

[2] Gerhard Kittel and Gerhard Friedrich, eds., *Theological Dictionary of the New Testament* 6 (Grand Rapids: William B. Eerdmans, 1968), pp. 878–879.

[3] Donald W. Richardson, *The Revelation of Jesus Christ* (Richmond: John Knox Press, 1939), p. 67.

[4] Edgar Young Mullins, *The Christian Religion in Its Doctrinal Expression* (Nashville: Baptist Sunday School Board, 1917), p. 347.

[5] Frank Stagg, *New Testament Theology* (Nashville: Broadman Press, 1962), p. 88.

5 / The Religious Axiom

All Men Have an Equal Right to Direct Access
to God

The meaning of this axiom is so clear that at first glance one might think that no discussion is needed beyond stating its self-evident truth. That all men have an equal right to access or a way of approach to God will scarcely be questioned by anyone. So the burden of the matter lies in the word *direct*. There should be no institution, human person, rite, or system which stands between the individual person and God. This axiom throws light upon the path that leads to the Father's heart and forbids anyone to place a stumbling block therein.

This axiom simply asserts the inalienable right of every person to deal with God for himself. It implies, of course, man's capacity to commune with God. It assumes the likeness between God and man. It is based upon the principle of the soul's competency in religion. It asserts that on the question of spiritual privilege there are no such differences in human nature as warrant our drawing a line between men and claiming for one group in this particular what cannot be claimed for others. It denies that there are any obstacles to any believing soul to any part of the Father's grace. There can, therefore, be no special classes in religion. All have equal access to the Father's table, the Father's ear, and the Father's heart.

Conversely, this religious axiom implies and carries with it the truth that to deprive any soul of the privilege of direct access to God is to place a man or an institution between the soul and God who created it. For one to assume the religious privilege or obligation of another is a contradiction in terms. Religion by its very nature forbids such assumption.

This fact does not forbid the setting apart of those who are chosen to render some special service to God within the fellowship of the church.

Neither does it deny the responsibility which the Bible places upon God's people to pray for and witness to the lost or one Christian to help with another's burden (cf. Gal. 6:2). Indeed, Jesus clearly told Peter that after passing through his ordeal of denying his Lord, he was to strengthen his brethren out of that experience (Luke 22:32). And the author of Hebrews exhorted his readers to be careful in helping troubled or weak brethren (12:12–13).

Only when church leaders presume to monopolize for themselves authority and privileges or when they usurp spiritual authority to become lords over the faith and life of others is there violation of this axiom. It ever stands as a warning to those who would invade the spiritual duties and rights of others.

Individualism in Religion

This axiom asserts the principle of individualism in religion. It is not to be interpreted apart from the person's obligation to society. But it does declare that primarily the religious relation is one between God and the individual person. Religious privilege and religious duty subsist between men and God in the first instance in their capacity as individuals and only secondarily in their social relations. However, on the social side of their religious life there is nothing which can properly claim the right to destroy the freedom of direct access which all people have to God or in any way to mar that fellowship. This is true whether the hindrance to direct access is a system of political government or of an authoritative church.

Direct access to God through Christ is inherent in the Christian faith. To seek to deny it to one person is spiritual and/or political tyranny. Jesus said, "No man cometh unto the Father, but by [through] me" (John 14:6). "Neither is there salvation in any other: for there is none other name under heaven given among men, whereby we must be saved" (Acts 4:12). "Therefore let no man glory in men. For all things are yours . . . and ye are Christ's; and Christ is God's" (1 Cor. 3:21,23)—literally, "And ye are of Christ, and Christ is of God." It is through Christ that man has direct access to God.

Nature of God and Man

This principle of direct access grows out of the very nature of both God and man. It is evident in the creation of man. The account of creation in Genesis 1 relates that repeatedly the creative acts of God below the human level were seen by him as good. But when he created man he saw that the entire creation was "very good" (Gen. 1:31). That which added emphasis to the goodness was man.

God is a person. As such he could not have fellowship with rocks, trees, mountains, oceans, or solar systems. He could have fellowship only with another person. And finite though he was/is, man was the crowning act of God's creative work. At the human level God created Eve to be a "help meet" to Adam (Gen. 2:18). The Hebrew word means one corresponding to him. Man himself was created as one corresponding to God, even though it was a correspondence of the finite to the infinite.

"So God created man in his own image, in the image of God created he him; male and female created he them" (Gen. 1:27). Since God is spiritual in essence, "image" cannot be construed as a physical likeness. It can only refer to the fact that finitely man possesses in his nature that which is infinite in God. "Image" means that man possesses self-conscious reason; he is a free being and "is capable of fellowship with God. Therein, above all other things, lies his peculiar dignity and privilege." [1]

As God is Spirit so man possesses a spiritual nature. As infinite Person God can approach the finite person. And man is capable of responding to God's approach, whether that response be positive or negative. But the fact remains that man as a spiritual person has a capacity for God. Indeed, man is never satisfied apart from God. "As the hart panteth after the water brooks, so panteth my soul after thee, O God. My soul thirsteth for God, for the living God" (Ps. 42:1–2). Even in the most wicked of hearts there is an echo of what that person might have been—what, indeed, in his deeper self he wants to be.

It is in the light of man's kinship with God that we find the rationale for the temptation of Adam and Eve (Gen. 3). Though man was a spiritual person, there was one element lacking. Man was not yet *righteous*. He was created in a state of innocence but with a tendency toward sin. However, he could not be righteous until he had refused the opportunity to be unrighteous. Had our primeval parents chosen to obey God's will rather than that of Satan, the oneness of fellowship would have been perfected.

But the tragic story is too familiar to need recounting. However, note one thing. The serpent's prize temptation was in the realm of spiritual ambition. Psalm 8:5 reads, "For thou hast made him a little lower than the angels" (KJV). The Hebrew word is not "angels" but "God" (*Elohim,* cf. Gen. 1:1). In Genesis 3:5 the same word is translated "gods." We are justified in reading this as "God." God made man a little lower than *God;* sin lies in man's effort to be *God.* It was at this point that our primeval parents became unrighteous rather than righteous.

When man sinned, the fellowship between him and God was broken; the divine image in man was marred. Yet no sooner did this tragedy occur but that God began the long process of restoring that fellowship (Gen. 3:15). And from that point on the story of the Bible is God's manifold effort to make possible reconciliation whereby once again man might be brought back into God's intended oneness of fellowship, and that in a state of righteousness, righteousness in Christ.

Covenants and Direct Access

The right of direct access to God involves responsibility as well as privilege. However we may explain it, under the Mosaic covenant the idea of family and community responsibility for sin arose. Achan's sin in taking spoils of war led to the initial defeat of Israel at Ai (Josh. 7). To remove the guilt Achan, his daughters, and his property were destroyed. Eventually children blamed their sins upon their forebears. But in Ezekiel 18:1–4 Jehovah reminded his people that sin and guilt were an individual matter. "What mean ye, that ye use this proverb concerning the land of Israel, saying, The fathers have eaten sour grapes, and the children's teeth are set on edge?" (v. 2). Earlier in the same vein in Jeremiah 31:29–30 the Lord said, "But every one shall die for his own iniquity: every man that eateth the sour grape, his teeth shall be set on edge'' (v. 30).

Immediately thereafter Jehovah announced a new covenant (Jer. 31:31–34). The author of Hebrews said that this new covenant replacing the old Mosaic covenant is fulfilled in Christ (Heb. 8). Under this new covenant every Christian is a priest. ''And they shall not teach every man his neighbour, and every man his brother, saying, Know the Lord: for all shall know me, from the least to the greatest'' (Heb. 8:11).

This does not mean that Christians should not witness to the lost or be concerned about their neighbor or Christian brother. The figure back of this is the Aaronic priesthood. Under this system an Israelite could approach God only through a priest. The priest told him what sacrifices to make for certain sins. And he was dependent upon the priest and his ministry if he was to approach God and receive forgiveness for his sins. But under the new covenant each Christian is his own priest. He has direct access to God through his own faith in Jesus Christ, who is the once-for-all sacrifice for sin (Heb. 4:14–16).

In considering covenants it is well to distinguish between God's covenant with Abraham (Gen. 12:1–3) and the one through Moses with Israel (Ex. 19:1–8). The latter was a covenant of law that involved Israel being a priest-nation to lead pagan peoples to worship and serve Jehovah. It was a *conditional* covenant, as noted by ''if'' and ''then'' (Ex. 19:5). Until the lesser party, Israel, fulfilled the condition, God, the greater party, was not bound by the promise. This covenant was sealed in animal blood (Ex. 24). When it became evident that Israel would not keep the covenant, God promised the new covenant of Jeremiah 31:31–34 (cf. Heb. 8; Matt. 21:33–45; 1 Pet. 2:1–10).

On the other hand, the covenant with Abraham was one of grace with no conditions attached. It was not sealed in animal blood. Hebrews 9:1 to 10:21 shows that this covenant was sealed in the blood of Christ. Its outgrowth is the *new covenant*. This Abrahamic covenant is the ''everlasting'' covenant of grace.

Scriptural Basis of This Axiom

The New Testament abounds in teachings that support the right of every person for direct access to God. Some have already been cited. We can examine only a few others, but they are representative of all. The emphasis in the New Testament is upon salvation through a direct experience with God through faith in Jesus Christ. It calls for a personal faith in Jesus on the part of the one being saved (John 1:12; 3:15–16,18,36; 5:24; 6:36,47; 11:25–26; Acts 10:43; 16:31; Rom. 1:16; 3:22,26; 4:3; 1 Cor. 1:21; 2 Tim. 1:12).

By the proof-text method some seek to inject baptism (administered by another person) as a requirement for salvation. But in Acts 2:38, for example, "for" (*eis*) may be translated variously. In Matthew 12:41 and Luke 11:32 it reads "at." The men of Nineveh did not repent in order that Jonah might preach, but as the result of his preaching. "As the result of" is a good rendering of *eis* in Acts 2:38. We use "for" in this sense. A man is executed *for* murder—not in order that he might murder, but as the result of murder already committed.

In 1 Peter 3:21 "baptism" (*baptisma*) means not the act of baptism, but the meaning in the act (death, burial, resurrection). Noah and his family were not saved by being *in* the water. They *were saved through* (*diesōthēsan,* note *dia,* through) the water by being in the ark, a type of Christ. The proof-text method is the weakest of all methods in interpretation. These examples are in direct conflict with the overall teaching of the New Testament.

At the Jerusalem Conference (Acts 15), as previously noted, the problem was salvation of the Gentiles. In the house of Cornelius, a Roman, Peter had seen the evidence that Gentiles were saved by believing in the gospel message, without benefit of a priest, circumcision, or any ritual of Judaism (Acts 10:44). At his return to Jerusalem he was called upon to justify his act of entering a Gentile's home (Acts 11:1–17). Upon hearing of his experience the brethren "held their peace, and glorified God, saying, Then hath God also to the Gentiles granted repentance unto life" (v. 18).

Later at the Jerusalem Conference Peter spoke to the matter at hand. After an obvious reference to his experience in Caesarea, he made an astounding statement. "But we believe that through the grace of the Lord Jesus Christ we [Jews] shall be saved, even as they [Gentiles]"

(Acts 15:11). The Judaizers were saying that Gentiles must become Jews in religion, through acts involving a priestly function, and then believe in Jesus for salvation. Peter, in effect, said, "You have the thing backwards. It is not that Gentiles must be saved as *Jews*. But we Jews must be saved the same way they are saved—by grace through faith in the Lord Jesus Christ." God has only one plan of salvation.

In Philippi Paul did not tell the Philippian jailer (a Roman) to join the church, to be baptized, or to partake of the Lord's Supper. He said, "Believe on the Lord Jesus Christ, and thou shalt be saved" (Acts 16:31).

One of the most potent passages in this regard is found in Ephesians 2:11–19. Paul was speaking of God's purpose in Christ to make of all men with their human differences one new man in Christ. The two great divisions in the Roman Empire were Jews and Gentiles. Of such Paul said, "For he [Christ] is our [Jew and Gentile] peace, who hath made both one and hath broken down the middle wall of partition" (v. 14). This "middle wall" refers to the fact that in the Jerusalem Temple Gentiles were not permitted to go beyond the court of the Gentiles. On the wall alongside each entrance from that court into the court of the Women [Jewish women] was placed a large stone on which were inscribed words forbidding Gentiles to go beyond that point upon the penalty of death (Acts 21:28–29). One of these stones has been found intact and is in a museum in Istanbul. A piece of another has been found.

These middle walls of partition forbade the Gentiles the right of access to God, who was said to dwell in the holy of holies in mercy with his people. In Ephesians 2:18 Paul said, "For through him [Christ] we both [Jew and Gentile] have access by one Spirit unto the Father." Regardless of one's race, class, or other condition, in Christ alone by the Holy Spirit he has the right to direct access to the Father.

Even for Jews, only the high priest could enter the holy of holies, and that only annually on the Day of Atonement. Before even he could do this he had to cleanse himself, don sacred clothes, and enter with the blood of the animal sacrifice. But when Jesus died on the cross "the veil of the temple [separating the Holy of Holies from the Holy Place] was

rent in twain from the top to the bottom'' (Matt. 27:51). Not from the
bottom to the top as if done by men, but from the top to the bottom—an
act of God! Thus all men through Christ have *direct* access to God (Heb.
9:1–15, 22–26; cf. 4:14–16).

In the Ephesians passage Paul spoke of how Christ has made it
possible for Gentiles as well as Jews to come directly to God. He
climaxed this with the words: "Now therefore *ye* [Gentiles] are no more
strangers and foreigners, but fellowcitizens with the saints [Christians],
and of the household of God'' (v. 19). In Christ they are not only
citizens of the kingdom of God; they also as God's children dwell in the
Father's house. And this by grace through faith in Christ, without
benefit of priest, ritual, or legalism.

These and other teachings of Scripture simply give in striking form
from the New Testament itself the essential contents of this religious
axiom. They disclose to us the peculiar and distinctive quality of
Christianity as a religion which asserts as inviolable the direct relation
of the soul to God. It naturally follows, therefore, that certain things are
excluded from Christianity by virtue of its essential nature. One is the
assumption on the part of one person of the religious obligations of
another. There can be no proxy religious experience. One person cannot
act in the place of another in so intimate an experience between the soul
and God. One person cannot breathe, drink, or eat for another person.
Likewise, a person cannot repent, confess, believe, and obey the Lord
for another.

The closest of human ties is that of the family. But one is not a
Christian simply because he has Christian parents or is married to a
Christian. Neither can family ties stand between a person and his access
to God. Jesus said that one's relation to God precedes such ties. "He
that loveth father or mother more than me is not worthy of me: and he
that loveth son or daughter more than me is not worthy of me'' (Matt.
10:37). "Loveth'' here carries the idea of choice (cf. Matt. 8:21–22).
"For whosoever shall do the will of my Father which is in heaven, the
same is my brother, and sister, and mother'' (Matt. 12:50).

Violations in Historical Christianity

Much of the material which comes under this heading has been treated earlier. Paganism, Gnosticism, Judaism, and Roman imperialism were the four principal forces contributing to the violation of this axiom. Weak and carnal Christians recently won out of paganism or Judaism tended to bring some of their former practices with them. Gnosticism's rites came to color the meaning and administration of the ordinances of baptism and the Lord's Supper. And as previously pointed out, the power structure of the Roman Empire is reflected in the hierarchical priesthood in the later church. Rites and ceremonies and the priestly system of the Old Testament also contributed to these violations.

Jesus himself warned against such a practice with regard to Judaism and Christianity. In so doing he laid down a principle which applies to the other elements contributing to these violations. "Neither do men put new wine into old bottles [wineskins]: else the bottles break, and the wine runneth out, and the bottles perish: but they put new wine into new bottles, and both are preserved" (Matt. 9:17). New wine tended to give off a gas which would cause old, dry wineskins to break. New wineskins would stretch with the increased volume. The lesson is that the "new wine" of the greater Christian revelation cannot be expressed in the structure of Judaism.

Also, when James and John requested privileged positions in the kingdom (Mark 10:35–41), Jesus gave the true nature of greatness in his kingdom. Pagan rulers in tyranny lorded it over their subjects (v. 42). But Jesus said literally, "But not so is it among you: but whosoever may will to become great among you, shall be your minister [diakonos, the lowest order of slaves]. And whosoever may will to be first among you shall be servant [doulos, slave] of all" (Mark 10:43–44). Jesus gave himself as the supreme model of this truth (v. 45). Pagan values regard as great the one who is served by the most people. Christian values regard one great who serves the most people. The kingdom standard is not human lordship but Christian servanthood.

These two teachings of Jesus apply directly to the matter at hand; for the perversion of Christian truth is evident in greater degree in episcopacy, sacerdotalism (priestly system and functions), and sacramentarian value applied to the ordinances than anywhere else. These may be summed up in the terms of ecclesiastical imperialism and sacramentalism. Of course, strictly speaking, episcopacy refers to government, and priests administer the sacraments. But the two offices actually overlap.

In the pagan mind direct and immediate relations between God and man seemed inconceivable—hence their priesthood. While this was to a much lesser degree the case in the Old Testament system, the priesthood was necessary in ritual and ceremony. And the priesthood of Judaism made the pagan idea more acceptable to the early Christians. All of these tendencies combined to obscure the one sufficient sacrifice, the priesthood of Jesus only as the author of salvation, and the universal priesthood of believers as the recipients of salvation.

These violations did not occur in a day or even in a generation, but gradually and finally they bore their bitter fruit. The priesthood became the repository of the mysteries and the grace of God. The hierarchy slowly evolved. The church consists of the hierarchy, and outside the church is no salvation. Thus the church, priesthood, and sacraments (which grew from two to seven) are all interposed between the soul and God. Faith passed into a long eclipse. Direct relations to God were unknown. Forgiveness became absolution; prayer became confession to a priest. Regeneration took place in baptism which was administered in infancy, lest death ensue before the sacrament was applied. The simple Lord's Supper became a Mass with its *Host* or the actual presence of the body and blood of Christ in the ritual.

The great elemental truth that all souls have an equal right to direct access to God passed out of human thought insofar as the Roman Catholic Church was able to influence that thought. Luther's Reformation was not directed primarily at the evils within the church but against spiritual tyranny. Yet some of its features stayed with the reformers, as seen in infant baptism, sacramental views of the ordinances, and episcopacy or related forms of church government. In the light of such misinterpretations of New Testament truth, three basic factors need to be reviewed.

Christ Jesus the Only Mediator

The picture of Jesus Christ as our one mediator is most clearly expressed in 1 Timothy 2:5. "For there is one God, and one mediator between God and men, the man Christ Jesus." Note that this one mediator is a man, not a woman; and there is but one mediator, not many. This rules out the traditional roles of Mary and/or the saints in this regard.

A mediator (*mesitēs*) was one appointed by a judge to mediate a difference between two parties. He must perfectly represent both, and he must do all that is necessary to bring them together. We have noted previously that God needs no reconciliation to man. It is man who needs to be reconciled to God. Now Paul said that Christ Jesus is the mediator appointed to effect this reconciliation.

The order "Christ Jesus" is not accidental. While "Christ" means the anointed one, it is also used here in the sense of the eternal Christ—involving his nature as God. Jesus is his human name, which means "Jehovah is salvation." "Of God and of men" may be seen in the sense of partaking of the nature of both God and man, apart from sin. So as deity Christ perfectly represents God. As humanity Jesus perfectly represents man. In his death and resurrection he has done all that is necessary to provide the grounds of salvation or reconciliation. Therefore, it is in the "one mediator," partaking of the nature of both God and man, that God and man meet in reconciliation. Thus in Christ Jesus man has the right to direct access to God (cf. Eph. 2:18).

Salvation by Grace Through Faith

This was the message preached by Paul and others to both Jews and Gentiles. Because of Christ's mediatorship, the entire human race may be saved. This does not mean universal salvation. Redemption from sin is offered to all people, but it is effected only in those who receive Christ as their Savior. Because salvation comes by grace through faith, all men have the right to direct access to God.

The verb form for "grace" (*charidzomai*) is used twenty-three times in the New Testament, fifteen times in Paul's letters. It is variously rendered in the King James Version as "forgive," "give," "freely give," "deliver," "grant," and "frankly forgive." But in each instance it may read "grace," such as "he [graced] them both" (Luke

7:42). The noun form (*charis*) is used 156 times. It is translated "grace" 130 times. It may refer to saving grace, to sustaining grace, or to the gift of a specific ministry such as Paul's calling as the apostle to the Gentiles. The context must decide in each case. The emphasis at this point is upon saving grace.

Perhaps the clearest expression of God's saving grace is found in Ephesians 2:8–10. "For by grace are ye saved through faith; and that not of yourselves: it is the gift of God: not of works, lest any man should boast. For we are his workmanship, created in Christ Jesus unto good works, which God hath before ordained that we should walk in them."

The basic idea of grace is to make a gift. In succession it meant to forgive a debt, a wrong, and, finally, a sin. Thus, insofar as redemption is concerned, it means that God's forgiveness is a gift of his grace. And it comes to a person "through [the channel of his] faith." With two emphatic negatives Paul said that it is most certainly "not out of yourselves . . . not out of works" (literal). "Out of" expresses source. Thus the source of this gift is neither one's own power nor his merit. The former of these negative statements may read, "And you have not done this of your own strength; it is a gift of God." [2] The same idea is present in the latter phrase. Thus redemption does not stem from one's innate power or from works done by or to a person by other human persons. The passive voice of "have ye been saved" (literal) means that it results from what another—in this case God in Christ—has done for a person.

Redeemed souls are the product of God's work alone. The verb "to create" in the Bible is never used of man's work, only of God's work. "Therefore if any man be in Christ, he is a new creature [creation]" (2 Cor. 5:17): "created in (*en*, in the sphere of] Christ Jesus." Good works are the *fruit,* not the *root,* of salvation. But even here they are the fruit of God's grace.

These verses are at the heart of the gospel. It is understandable, therefore, why Paul so vehemently opposed the teachings of the Judaizers, which involved both a priestly function and legalism (Gal. 1:6–9; cf. Acts 15:1). He said that it is not "another" (*allo*) of the same kind of gospel which Paul preached (v. 7). Indeed, it is not a gospel at all.

"Gospel" means "good news," or what God in Christ has done for man's salvation. God is constant in behavior and nature (Mal. 3:6; Heb. 13:8). But man is so erratic in nature and conduct that if in any sense his salvation depends upon him or another human being—then the teaching of the Judaizers is bad news. Of interest is the fact that those who teach that one can be saved and then lost again also teach a salvation by works *plus* faith. Those who hold to the security of the believer preach a gospel of salvation by grace *through* faith. We must be careful to point out the security belongs to the *believer,* not the *church member.*

Inherent in salvation by grace through faith is the concept of the right of direct access to God. The lost sinner may approach God without personal merit or the ministrations of any church, priest, or potentate. No ordinance stands between him and the fountain of living waters. No requirement or ministry of man—political or ecclesiastical—bars the way of a repentant sinner to stand before God. He stands for himself in awesome responsibility before him in whose omniscience all souls are bared. If he remains lost, it is by his own choice. If he is saved, it is by God's grace through the channel of a personal faith in and commitment to God in Christ. If he truly repents, he will believe. Repentance and faith are inseparable graces.

In laying down the one human requirement of personal faith, God has set the condition which all people can meet. Every person exercises faith. It is simply a question of what or who is the object of faith: money, self-righteousness, heritage, or God in Christ. Literally, Paul said, "For I know [in] whom I have believed" (2 Tim. 1:12).

Priesthood of Believers

Already we have noted that under the new covenant (Heb. 8) every Christian is a priest with Jesus Christ as our High Priest (Heb. 4:14; 9:11). Under the old covenant the tribe of Levi was the priestly tribe which ministered on behalf of the other eleven tribes. In Revelation 5:10 the redeemed in heaven praise the Lamb who "hast made us unto our God kings and priests" or a *royal priesthood.* In Exodus 19:6 at the making of the Mosaic or old covenant Israel was to be a "kingdom of priests." Thus Israel was chosen not merely for privilege but for a priestly service for God to the pagan nations. God did not choose Israel because he loved her more than other people. Because he loves all people, he chose Israel as his priest-nation to them (Ex. 19:5).

In Matthew 21:33–43, after describing Israel's repeated failure to honor her covenant, Jesus said that "the kingdom of God shall be taken from you, and given to a nation bringing forth the fruits thereof" (v. 43). In 1 Peter 2:1–10 the apostle combined the language of Exodus 19 and Matthew 21 to show that the new Israel is composed of those who believe in Christ. "Ye also, as lively stones, are built up a spiritual house, an holy priesthood, to offer up spiritual sacrifices, acceptable to God by [through] Jesus Christ" (v. 5). And in this new Israel every believer is a priest, involving both privilege and responsibility.

The privileges include the right to read and interpret the Scriptures for oneself under the leadership of the Holy Spirit, to pray directly to God through Jesus Christ, and to confess one's sins to God directly without the aid of any human mediator. These are inherent in the principle of the competency of the soul in religion. The responsibility, of course, is to share the gospel with all men and to be a good steward of both life and substance.

The priesthood of believers is a precious article of faith among Baptists. But sometimes in their zeal for biblical truth as a certain person or group understands it, they tend to violate its very principle. With respect to interpreting the Scriptures, each *priest* has the right to do so as he is led by the Holy Spirit. The fact that at times two persons may arrive at different conclusions is due to the fallibility of man. The amazing thing, however, is not that Baptists have doctrinal differences, but that they have so few.

The article on "The Scriptures" in *The Baptist Faith and Message* closes with "The criterion by which the Bible is to be interpreted in Jesus Christ." This statement is not a creed binding upon the conscience, but an effort to set forth those things generally believed among Southern Baptists. The Preamble to this statement is careful to guard the competency of the soul in religion. When one Baptist or group of such tries to coerce another to dot every *i* and cross every *t* as he does, he violates the priesthood of believers, the competency of the soul in religion. To ignore the Preamble is to deny Baptist autonomy.

Baptists and Direct Access

As stated at the outset, Christians of all persuasions agree that every man has the right of direct access to God. Believers differ however, on the word *direct*. Roman Catholicism would erase this word altogether. Those who retain some elements derived from that system, in varying degrees, tend to tone down the *direct* concept. Certainly infant baptism for whatever reason clouds the issue. Where salvation is made dependent upon human merit or any *priestly* function, such as the administration of ordinances, it is a denial of the direct concept. Episcopacy and its related systems raise a question at this point.

The record of Baptists is clear and clean in this regard. In their teachings not even a shadow of non-New Testament principles or practices falls across the path of direct access to God. Because of their name and their insistence upon retaining the New Testament mode of baptism, some non-Baptists think that Baptists believe in baptismal regeneration. Nothing could be farther from the truth. Strangely, now and then some Baptist seems to believe this. On occasion I have heard one say, "I am so glad he was baptized before he died!" Or someone will express regret that a person was not baptized—which only shows that uninformed Baptists are susceptible to absorbing some of the *atmosphere* of other groups among whom they live. The insistence of Baptists upon believer's baptism only is clear proof that this is not the case of Baptists generally; nor is it found in their doctrinal statements.

The noncreedal nature of Baptists and their insistence that every person has the right to read and interpret the Scriptures for himself does at times lead to diverse views. Indeed, even these tensions are evidence of a living faith. If a muscle loses its tension it loses its usefulness. A faith that does not present tensions is evidence of a stereotyped creedal faith void of a *living* nature.

Throughout their recorded history Baptists have ever been the champions of every person's right of direct access to God. This is evident in their denial of any one person, ecclesiastical system, political entity, rite or ceremony's standing between the soul and God. The mediatorship of

Christ, salvation by grace through faith, and the priesthood of believers are the positive expressions of Baptists' faithfulness to this axiom. Other Christian groups may/do hold to some or even all of the meaning of this axiom. But Baptists historically and in the present are its leading champions. They invite all Christians to examine their positions in light of New Testament truth. It is only in this light that Christians can fully obey the climax of the Bible's multiple invitations to come to God through Christ.

One day during a crusade in Oklahoma City Billy Graham spoke to a joint meeting of civic clubs. His message was a simple sermon on salvation by grace through faith in Jesus Christ. At the close non-Baptist men whom I knew to hold positions of leadership in their churches, comparable to the office of deacon, rushed forward to thank Billy for his message. More than once they were heard to say, "I have been going to church all my life, but I never heard that before. It is the greatest thing I ever heard!" The Baptist governor of Oklahoma said to me, "You know, preacher, they could hear a similar sermon on any given Sunday in any Baptist church in Oklahoma. But they do not know it is there."

Truly we need to proclaim that every man has the right of direct access to God. It underlies the very heart of the Christian gospel.

Notes

[1] Herschel H. Hobbs, *The Origin of All Things* (Waco: Word Books, 1975), p. 31.

[2] William F. Arndt and F. Wilbur Gingrich, *A Greek-English Lexicon of the New Testament* (Cambridge: University Press, 1957), p. 21.

6 / The Ecclesiastical Axiom

All Believers Have a Right to Equal Privileges
in the Church

At the outset it is well to note that this axiom, while teaching equality of privilege in the local church, has no reference to differences in the mental and spiritual capacities of people. No one regards all people as possessing equal natural ability of intellect. Nor does this axiom assume that one person is as well fitted as another for official position in the church. Diversities of gifts, offices, and administrations are clearly recognized in the New Testament churches (1 Cor. 12:4–11).

However, it is also true that competency in the economic world does not automatically qualify one for a place of like responsibility and leadership in the church. It is possible that through greater spiritual development a bank clerk may be better qualified to lead in the Lord's work than a bank president. But with equal spiritual commitment the latter has more to offer in some positions than the former.

Nevertheless, the substance of this axiom is that all Christians have a right to equal privileges in the church. No one believer should enjoy special privilege or sit in authority over another fellow believer, for only Jesus Christ is Lord.

Ecclesiastical and Religious Axioms Related

The ecclesiastical axiom flows naturally from the religious axiom. Since people have an equal right of access to God, they also are entitled to equal privileges in the church. Equality before God makes men equal in their ecclesiastical standing. The church is a brotherhood; it is a family of which God is the Father and Jesus Christ is the elder brother. With respect to the people in the church, there is no law of primogeniture by which favored sons receive special and disproportionate parts of the Father's inheritance; there is no law of hereditary lordship by which spiritual dynasties are established through the laying on of hands or otherwise.

The methods of the church are those of a spiritual brotherhood of equals. Personal adjustment of offenses, not judicial decisions, is Christ's preferred way in all private grievances; and nowhere does he establish a court other than the local congregation (Matt. 5:23–26; 18:15–17). Paul echoed these truths in 1 Corinthians 6:1–8. Even apostles, who were especially empowered for their tasks, exerted their authority not as lords of the conscience but as brothers. Furthermore, the idea of apostolic succession is tradition, not Scripture.

Twofold Relationship of the Believer

The nature of Christ's church is determined by the twofold relationship of the believer—one to Christ himself, the other to the brethren.

Christ is Lord. The believer belongs to an absolute monarchy, the most absolute indeed the world ever knew (Matt. 28:18; Rev. 19:16). But the Monarch is in heaven and relates himself to his subjects through his revealed Word and through his Spirit. The subject has fellowship directly with the Monarch. All his dealings with his subjects are individual. He delegates his authority to none. But the first and finest expression of Christ's lordship over the individual believer is in the gift of autonomy. Christ discovers each man for himself and starts him on an autonomous career, but never for a moment does he relax his grasp upon that person's conscience or life. Obviously this is a paradox: the lordship of Christ and the autonomy of the believers.

Now because the individual deals directly with his Lord and is immediately responsible to him, the spiritual society must be a democracy. That is, the church is a community of autonomous individuals under the immediate lordship of Christ held together by a common faith and inspired by a common task and ends, all of which are assigned to him by the one Lord. The church, therefore, is the expression of the paradoxical conception of the union of *absolute monarchy* and *pure democracy*. Every form of church polity other than democracy somewhere infringes upon the lordship of Christ. I mean *direct* lordship. There is no indirect lordship known to the New Testament. An ecclesiastical monarchy with a human head radically alters the very nature of Christianity. Baptist congregationalism is the exact antithesis of the Romish hierarchy. Modified ecclesiastical monarchies, aristocracies, or oligarchies are less objectionable; but they too violate one or the other of the organic laws of the church, the direct lordship of Christ, or the equality of all believers in spiritual privilege.

It is a logical conclusion, therefore, that pure democracy in church polity is the only institutional expression, the only expression in the form of church organization, of the religious axiom—the soul's right to dealing with God—and the ecclesiastical axiom—the equality of believers in spiritual privilege in the church. It thus appears that the question of church polity is more than a few detached proof texts from the New Testament. The question of the constitution of the church enters vitally into the question of the constitution of the kingdom of God. This is not to equate the church with the kingdom. But the King of the kingdom is also the Lord of the church. And as the believer has the right of direct access to the King, so he has the right to equal privileges in the church.

New Testament Pattern

While we should not resort to the proof-text method simply to prove a preconceived point, it is a legitimate approach to examine certain passages of Scripture in order to discern the overall pattern of New Testament churches. New Testament scholarship generally sees the churches of the first century as democratic bodies.

It may be conceded that at Pentecost under the guidance of the Holy Spirit the church in Jerusalem began to take an organizational form. However, in its most elementary concept the church existed from the moment that a small group of disciples gathered about Jesus. Eventually he chose twelve apostles for the purpose of training them so that they might discharge specific functions (Mark 3:13–15). In Mark 3:14 "ordained" reads "made" in the Greek text. This fact is noted simply to point out that in this early group there was no gradation of authority.

Because Peter always appears first in the lists of apostles (Matt. 10:2–4; Mark 3:16–19; Luke 6:14–16; Acts 1:13), some see him as the chief apostle. But there is no evidence of this in the New Testament.

Because of his outgoing nature he often spoke for the group. But the constant dispute as to which should be the greatest among them shows that the other apostles did not regard him as *chief*. Paul certainly had no such idea (Gal. 2:7,11–14). The church in Jerusalem held to no such position (Acts 11:18). Peter himself was under no such illusion, as seen in 1 Peter 5:1 when he referred to himself as a "fellow elder" with other elders. According to the record, he was never pastor or elder of a local church, but was a missionary or traveling evangelist. However, this shows that he entertained no idea of supremacy.

This same pattern of equality carries over into the large picture of the first-century churches. The two stated officers in a local church were pastors, bishops, or elders and deacons (Phil. 1:1). But the only *authority* they had was that of leadership and service. These elements are necessary even in a democracy, but to attach authority to these offices is to misread the New Testament.

"Deacon" comes from the Greek word *diakonos,* referring to the lowest kind of slave. Jesus performed one service of such a slave when he rinsed his disciples' feet (John 13:2–17). Quoting Jesus at the Last Supper, Luke 22:27 reads, "I am among you as he that serveth." The Greek text reads "as the one serving," using the participial form of the verb from *diakonos.*

The office of deacon probably stems from the selection of helpers for the apostles (Acts 6:1–6). But note that they were selected by the congregation. The name deacon does not appear. But the word rendered "ministration" is *diakoniai* (v. 1). And "serve" (v. 2) translates the present infinitive *diakonein.* So the office of deacon is not one of authority but of service.

In Acts 20:28 we see the offices of elder, bishop, and pastor (shepherd). In speaking to the Ephesian elders Paul said, "Take heed therefore unto yourselves, and to all the flock, over the which the Holy Ghost [Spirit] hath made you overseers [*episkopous,* bishops], to feed [as a shepherd, *poimanein*) the church of God." The term "elder" originally applied to old men who out of their wisdom could give counsel. In the New Testament in the Christian sense it applied to those in a church who gave wise counsel and leadership. The Greek word for *bishop* was used for one who oversaw the work of others to see that it was done properly. And the word for "shepherd" became *pastor* in the sense of a pastoral scene of a shepherd and his sheep.

The fact that there was a plurality of elders in the church in Ephesus and of bishops in the church in Philippi suggests that different ones did special work, much like the staff of a large church today. There may even have been a senior elder, bishop, or pastor in the same modern sense. But there is no suggestion of authority attached to the office. In no case in the New Testament was a bishop over a group of churches.

It should be noted that in Baptist church polity, there are men who exercise the function of leadership at various levels in the denominational structure. For instance, state conventions have executive secretaries. But while carrying out certain functions associated with the idea of *bishop* in some other denominations, the position carries with it no authority. These persons help to promote the work and correlate joint efforts of the various conventions. But none exercises authority over either the churches or the state convention. They are *servants,* not authorities.

The offices of pastor and deacon suggest the matter of ordination. The word "ordained" in John 15:16 simply means placed. In Acts 14:23 the word means to appoint. The Greek word means to stretch forth the hand as in voting, which suggests that these elders, as in the case of deacons, were elected by the churches rather than chosen by the apostles. They were then set apart for their work through prayer and the laying on of hands (Acts 6:6).

In churches today it is customary in ordination to lay on hands by the ordaining council. Mention of this practice is found in the New Testament (cf. Acts 13:3; note its absence in 14:23; 1 Tim. 4:14; 2 Tim. 1:6). In Acts 13:3 it is not clear whether the entire congregation or a smaller group acting for the congregation did this. But one thing is clear. Paul did not regard this as making him an apostle (Gal. 1:1). The purpose in Antioch was simply to set Barnabas and Saul apart to a special work to which the Holy Spirit had called them. The two references in letters to Timothy probably refer to the same thing. In the former instance the elders and Paul laid on hands. In the latter in a very personal letter Paul mentioned himself alone. The "gift of God" in each case was not some mystical grace or spiritual power otherwise unattainable. It most likely refers to the work God had given him to do in and about Ephesus. Least of all does it refer to authority over churches or other believers.

"From the few instances mentioned above (the only ones found in the NT), we infer that it was advisable that persons holding high office in the church should be publicly recognized in some way, as by laying on of hands, fasting, and public prayer. But no great emphasis was laid on this rite, hence it can hardly be likely that any essential principle was held to be involved in it" (Hort, *The Christian Ecclesia,* 216). It was regarded as an outward act of approval, a symbolic offering of intercessory prayer, and an emblem of the solidarity of the Christian community, rather than an indispensable channel of grace for the work of the ministry. [1]

However, as we have seen in other cases of perversion of New Testament truth, this simple practice soon came to be regarded as a means of bestowing special grace and authority upon the subject. But such a practice and meaning are foreign to the New Testament.

Four clear examples of democracy in the local church are found in Matthew 18:15–20; Acts 15; 1 Corinthians 5:4–5; and 1 Corinthians 16:3. The first example involves a matter of fellowship. When other efforts at reconciliation failed, the final recourse was to the local church. Note the order: (1) One Christian went to another who had some sort of misunderstanding with him. (2) When the latter refused to become reconciled, the former took others with him. (3) If this move failed, the matter was brought before the church. Verse 18 is heaven's authority for a local church to handle its own affairs. Verses 19–20 constitute Jesus' promise to be with the church to guide as it acts. It should act in the will of the Lord.

The second example where two local churches handled a doctrinal problem affecting both is the Jerusalem Conference. A careful analysis of Acts 15 shows a general meeting of the congregation (vv. 4–5), a committee meeting to study the matter (vv. 6–11), and a second congregational meeting to consider the report of the committee (vv. 12–29).

The third instance involves church discipline. The passive voice of "gathered together" (1 Cor. 5:4) suggests a call for an assembly of the church, perhaps coming from the moderator. They were then to act in the power of the Lord Jesus under the Holy Spirit's guidance.

The fourth case involved the selection by the church of those who were to take the relief offering to Jerusalem. In each instance the seat of local authority is the church, not the apostles or any other one person. Regarding personal relationships, moral conduct, and doctrinal matters, the problems were not submitted to civil courts or to an official body outside the involved churches. In 1 Corinthians 6:1–8 Paul chided members of that church for going into pagan civil courts to settle their differences. By inference he said that the church was able to handle such matters. A local church is a family. Problems within the family should be kept within the family, not aired before the entire community. They should be settled in love, not by law. In each of these cases, with the exception of 1 Corinthians 16:3, it is stated that the church acted under the authority of the Lord (cf. Matt. 18:18–19; Acts 15:28; 1 Cor. 5:4).

Perversion of the New Testament Pattern

In chapter 2 we noted that the shift from the New Testament pattern of democracy to an autocracy or the Roman Catholic hierarchy came about gradually. During all this time the Roman Catholic priesthood as we know it was being formed with ranks and grades of authority. In time the ordinances became sacraments said to have saving power. These were said to be effective only when administered by a priest under the authority of the bishop, later the papacy. The names *clergy* (those called of God) and *laity* (the people) removed any semblance of the believer's direct access to God and equal privileges within the church. [2] The tragic result of all this is seen in the previous chapter.

It should be noted that the New Testament does allow for growth in the organization of the churches, as seen in the mention of services other than those of pastors and deacons. But it was a change from *within*.

Growth from within is exactly the pattern of the New Testament. First came the call of Christ and the response of the individual. Then came groups of individuals attached to a person. When the Holy Spirit came at Pentecost, the current definition of the church began under the leadership of the Spirit. Believers were drawn together. The indwelling Spirit began to organize the membership of Christ's body into his church.

There was neither priest nor bishop in the medieval and modern sense of the terms in the New Testament churches. These were pure democracies. Democracy alone accords with the nature of the kingdom of God. Direct relations of men to God and their equality as brethren require a democratic church polity. No other polity leaves the soul free. Whenever men are acted upon directly by the spiritual environment, they tend toward the free and self-governing congregation.

A striking example of this is that of the beginning of modern Baptist work in Germany. Due to certain troubles falsely related to Anabaptists in the fifteenth century, the name *Baptist* was in ill repute in Germany. Johann Gerhardt Oncken, a German lad of fourteen, was taken to Great Britain by a Scottish merchant. There he was converted and joined a Congregational church. When he was twenty-three years old he returned to Germany as a missionary. Though successful in his work, he encountered strong opposition from the state church.

After some years of careful study of the Scriptures, Oncken became convinced that the baptism of believers only is taught in the New Testament and that only immersion is taught in the Scriptures.

In Mexico, Brazil, and elsewhere Baptist churches have sprung spontaneously into being, so to speak, as a result of the simple study of the New Testament under the sole tutelage of the Holy Spirit. I heard a missionary tell about finding a little church far into the interior, with little contact with the outside world. With no textbook except the New Testament they had formed a church which was functioning as do Baptist churches. Yet they did not know that *Baptist* churches existed. They had grown from within!

The elaborate Roman Catholic system was effected by forces from *without*—the geographical location of Rome, the Petrine tradition, the need for centralized authority to oppose heresy, the fall of the empire calling for some strong person about whom to rally, the heathen influence which affected the meaning of the ordinances, and both pagan and Jewish influence in the rise of the priesthood. In this case the temporal and political environment imposed its laws upon a spiritual body. Thus the church ceased to be an organism and became a mechanism. The individual and democracy were lost in the process. And in the Reformation, as in so many other cases, the church stopped at the halfway house where the individual became secondary and the center of authority became the *few* rather than the *many*.

We are now ready to examine certain facets of New Testament teaching concerning the church and the place of the individual in it. In each instance we shall see both the privilege and responsibility which rest upon every believer.

Christ and the Church

Though the word translated "church" is used 115 times in the New Testament, according to the Gospels Jesus used it only 3 times (for example, Matt. 16:18; 18:17). In the former reference he spoke of the church in general; in the latter he spoke of a local church.

Following Peter's confession of Jesus' messiahship as "the Christ, the Son of the living God," Jesus commended him for his reply, which could have come only from God. Then he spoke of his church. "And I say unto thee, That thou art Peter, and upon this rock I will build my church; and the gates of hell [hades, the abode of the dead] shall not prevail [have strength] against it. And I will give unto thee the keys of the kingdom of heaven: and whatsoever thou shalt bind on earth shall be bound in heaven: and whatsoever thou shalt loose on earth shall be loosed in heaven" (Matt. 16:18–19).

This is the first of three passages upon which Leo I based the claim of the papacy (see also Luke 22:31–32; John 21:15–17). In this claim emphasis was placed upon the singular "thou art Peter," as though Jesus spoke to him as a person. However, it may be insisted that as Peter spoke for the twelve (Matt. 16:15–16), Jesus replied to the twelve through Peter. In verses 18–19 let us note the foundation, nature, and mission of the church.

"Peter" translates the masculine Greek word *petros*. "Rock" renders the feminine word *petra*. The difference in gender forbids "rock" from referring to Peter. *Petra* connotes a large ledge rock such as the foundation stone of a building or a cliff. Such a rock may be seen today at the base of the cliff on which once stood the ancient city of Caesarea Philippi (Matt. 16:13). *Petros* means a small stone broken off of a *petra* and partaking of its nature. Some scholars insist that Jesus spoke in Aramaic, in which case this distinction would not apply. Perhaps so. But Matthew has recorded in Greek the substance of Jesus' words.

Various interpretations have been offered for verse 18: the rock is Peter, Peter and others who make his confession about Jesus as the Christ, the faith expressed, Christ himself. We have noted the grammatical problem with regard to Peter. The second interpretation is an adaptation of the first. The third bases the church upon an act of man. Those eliminations leave the view of Christ as the Son of the living God. G. Campbell Morgan says, "If we trace the figurative use of the word rock through the Hebrew Scriptures, we find that it is never used symbolically of man, but always of God." [4] His conclusion is that the church is founded upon God as revealed in Jesus Christ. But since he is God, it is sufficient to see Christ as the foundation as well as the head (Col. 1:18) of the church (1 Cor. 3:11). In 1 Peter 2:5 the apostle spoke of Christians as lively or living "stones . . . built up a spiritual house."

We may conclude, therefore, that Christ is "the church's one foundation." We, like Peter, are small stones that partake of Christ's nature and are being built into the superstructure. In 1 Peter 2:5 he used a different word for "stones" (*lithoi*), but this does not affect the ultimate meaning. Of further interest is the fact that in 1 Peter 5:3 the apostle admonished his fellow elders "neither as being lords [lording down] over God's heritage, but being ensamples to the flock." Not lords but examples!

The nature of the church is seen in "my church." So much energy and time have been expended in debate over the *foundation* and *keys* that interpreters have missed one fine point which is so vital. In Greek emphasis is determined by position in a sentence. For instance, where a pronoun precedes a noun, the emphasis is on the pronoun. In this case had Jesus said "the church of me," emphasis would be upon "church." But Jesus said "of me the church." So the emphasis is upon "my."

"Upon this rock I will build *my* church."

"Church" renders the Greek work *ekklēsia* (note "ecclesiastical") which means called-out ones or assembly. In Greek life it was used for a local political assembly of the citizens of a city. In Acts 19:39, 41 it is used in this sense. In the Roman Empire, as a reward for some service to the empire, certain cities were granted the status of "free" cities. Such a city was Ephesus. Among other things this involved a certain amount of local, democratic rule; but it was within the framework of the laws of the empire. We see this in the assembly in Ephesus.

In the Septuagint (Greek translation of the Old Testament) this word was used to translate *qahal,* the assembly of Israel before God in the wilderness, under his direct theocratic rule (Deut. 31:30). The word is used in this sense twice in the New Testament (Acts 7:38; Heb. 2:12). Thus the word had both a local, democratic meaning and a general theocratic meaning. In essence Jesus said, "The Gentiles have their assembly, and the Hebrews have their assembly. Now I am going to build *my* assembly." And, while distinct from them, Christ's church partakes of the nature of both.

In 93 of the 115 times that *ekklesia* is used in the New Testament, it refers to the local church. At times it refers to all the redeemed of all the ages (cf. Eph. 1:22–23; 3:10–11; Col. 1:18). The word is never used to refer to a group of churches. When more than one church is involved the plural form is used (cf. 2 Cor. 8:1; Gal. 1:2). So on the one hand we see the church general (Hebrew idea), a theocracy under the direct rule of God (Christ), and on the other hand we see the local church (Greek idea) as a democracy. But as the free cities enjoyed local rule within the framework of the laws of the Roman empire, so local churches operate through democratic processes but under the lordship of Jesus Christ. So we come again to the dual idea of an absolute monarchy and a local democracy. It is at this point that caution must be exercised.

Autonomy (self-rule) is a precious word to Baptists. But words, like people, can run in bad company. At times one may hear, "This is a Baptist church. It can do as it pleases!" Or, "I am a Baptist. I will do as I please!" This is not *autonomy* but *anarchy*. Both churches and Baptists must do as Christ pleases or wills. R. Paul Caudill suggests that the local church should be called a "Christocracy." This catches the sense of the absolute lordship of Christ. This is why *The Baptist Faith and Message* reads, "This church is an autonomous body, operating through democratic processes under the Lordship of Jesus Christ. In such a congregation all members are equally responsible." [5] Equal responsibility implies equal privilege.

Matthew 18:20 is usually read in the context of prayer. But its immediate context is that of a local church in a congregational meeting dealing with a problem of fellowship. Basically it promises the Lord's presence when a local church meets to transact his business (Matt. 28:20; John 14:16–18; 1 Cor. 5:4). The same applies in cooperative endeavor between local churches (Acts 15:28). The Holy Spirit did not *replace* Jesus; he is Jesus in spiritual presence in his people and churches. Christ said that it was expedient that he go away in order that the Holy Spirit might come (John 16:7). As someone said, he "exchanged his presence for his omnipresence."

If a local church, in prayerful business session and guided by the Holy Spirit, cannot find the Lord's will in a matter—then who can? Though the decision may be contrary to my wishes it is my responsibility, after having expressed my privilege in discussion of the matter, to abide by and cooperate in the course of action chosen.

Several years ago the First Baptist Church, Oklahoma City, Oklahoma, was considering a building program. At best the proposed building effort would leave the church with a debt of over 800,000 dollars. One influential and wealthy member favored a less pretentious program and a smaller debt. He so stated in numerous meetings. But when the church decided on the larger program, he came to me with the request that he be made chairman of a committee to raise the money to pay the debt. He himself gave one-tenth of the overall cost. Here is both privilege and responsibility as the Lord wills them to be used.

It should be noted also that the church is not a membership but a *fellowship*. The former term is not used in the New Testament with reference to church relationships. The word is fellowship (*koinonia*), a sharing or having all things in common. This applies to both privilege and responsibility. It is a fellowship effected by the Holy Spirit (1 Cor.

3:16; 12:13).

Regarding the church as a fellowship will correct many abuses concerning church relationship. If you live in one city and your name is on the roll of a church in another city, you are not *in fellowship*. Unless providentially hindered, you must be there in order to be in fellowship. If you habitually out of indifference absent yourself from the assembling of your church, you are not in fellowship. Even if you attend its services but are out of harmony with the pastor, deacons, teacher, and/or others in the body, you are not in fellowship. Jesus said that in such case you cannot even worship God properly (Matt. 5:23–24). And if you attend and avail yourself of the church's privileges but do not share in giving and service, you are not in full fellowship. Like grace, church fellowship offers its privileges, but it makes its demands.

Inherent in the axiom that all believers have equal rights within the church is the added matter of equal responsibilities to the degree that one can assume them. This truth is involved in Paul's words that as believers are heirs with Christ, they must also be sufferers with him. These truths entail being glorified ones with him (Rom. 8:17). A person is more likely to avail himself of his *rights* if he also bears his responsibilities.

Now a word about the mission of the church. Matthew 16:19 is one basis of papal claims with regard to the confessional and the forgiveness of sins. If this be true, then in Matthew 18:18 Christ invested the same power of retaining or loosing sins with the local church. Neither is true. Only God forgives sin/sins when in repentance, confession, and faith we come directly before him through Christ (Mark 2:7–12; 1 John 2:1). The papacy regards "keys" in a twofold sense, one as ecclesiastical and the other as political—thus the claim to rule in both areas. Even though the pope rules politically over only a few acres called the Vatican, this claim to dual rulership has never been withdrawn.

Jesus' phrase "keys of the kingdom of heaven" probably referred to the gospel. Jesus committed the gospel to his church. God's redemptive purpose centers in his churches (Eph. 3:10–11). Other more glamorous movements come and go. But until the Lord comes again, his churches will be in business for him. This is the sense of "the gates of hell [hades] shall not prevail against it'' (Matt. 16:18). Death or its realm will not destroy the church.

Unfortunately, most versions mistranslate verse 19 (see Williams and New American Standard Version for exceptions). Literally, the Greek text reads ''shall have been bound . . . shall have been loosed in heaven.'' It is not that an action taken by the church or any ecclesiastical power on earth will later be approved in heaven. Rather, heaven has already made a decree. The gospel is committed to Christ's churches. If they bind it on earth by not declaring it, heaven has no other plan by which to proclaim it. But if they loose it on earth many will hear; some will believe; and heaven has already decreed that all who believe will be saved. Every Christian should accept this glorious privilege and assume this awesome responsibility.

A careful study of Matthew 28:16–20 shows that the Great Commission was not given only to apostles. Among the group were others (note ''some doubted'' who had not yet seen Jesus after his resurrection) also. This probably includes the ''above five hundred'' of 1 Corinthians 15:6. So evangelism is ''every Christian's job.'' Equal privilege? Yes. But equal responsibility also.

Body of Christ

This term is often used to designate the church (cf. 1 Cor. 12:27; Eph. 1:23; Phil. 3:21; Col. 1:18,24). Indeed, it is the favorite term used. The church is the body of Christ with him as its head (Eph. 4:15–16). In one sense this refers to the church general, but it applies to the church local also.

In 1 Corinthians 12 when writing to a local church, Paul gave his marvelous analogy of the human body and the body of Christ. The church members are the members of the body of Christ. As its head Christ controls the body, even as the control center of the human body is the brain. The will issues its mandates directly to the members of the body, and in a properly functioning body they respond. Church members are members of Christ and of one another. Thus in the figure of the body we have a striking exposition of the twofold relationship of the believer which determines the nature of the church: a direct relation to the head and a relation of equality to other members of the body.

It is unnecessary to analyze 1 Corinthians 12 fully, but certain things should be noted. The heart of this chapter is that God in Christ by the Holy Spirit has given certain gifts and responsibilities to the various members of his body (vv. 4–14). No part of the body should despise any other part; no single Christian should see his role as less than that of others (vv. 15–25). All parts are necessary for the body to function properly. All are so related that what affects one affects all (v. 26). Each person should function in his own sphere (vv. 28–30), and all are to exercise their gifts in Christian love (1 Cor. 13).

No one person possesses all of the gifts of the Spirit. None should regard his gift as of more importance than those of others or vice versa. These gifts are *not* to be sought but received, developed, and used to the Lord's glory. The Holy Spirit distributes "to every man severally as he will" (v. 11).

Here then is a picture of equal privileges in the church. If one does not exercise his gift/gifts, he is at fault, not God. The *charisma* or gifts of grace are not reserved for the few but are given to all as the Spirit wills. No one person or group of persons is to deny to another his right of expression. But every Christian is responsible for using his gift as God intends. You cannot separate privilege and responsibility other than to note that the church body should not deny the privilege and the person should not shirk the responsibility. Each church and person should examine its/his own practice to determine how each measures up to this New Testament pattern.

Many years ago I read a treatment of the body of Christ which compared it to a pipe organ. An organ has many pipes of various sizes, each with its own note. Some pipes peep like birds; others rumble like thunder. But each is important in its place. It is the proper combination of tones which produces beautiful music. These tones are made as wind rushes through the pipes, in response to the organist's pressing of keys and pedals.

Now just suppose that a little pipe should say, "I am so small. My little tone is drowned out by the louder ones. So when the organist presses my key I will not play." The audience would marvel at the music. But the organist, whose ear is trained to catch every tone, would say, "The little pipe did not play."

We are similar pipes in the giant pipe organ of God. Each must perform as the Holy Spirit, the wind of God, passes through us. The Spirit does this as Christ, the master organist, presses the keys and pedals of our wills. But just suppose that one "little pipe" decided not to respond. The world would say, "That church is doing a great work!" But Christ would say, "The little pipe did not play!"

For their purposes there are no big or little pipes. Each is important in its place. When all the pipes in God's organ respond to the will of Christ through the Holy Spirit, their tones blend into beautiful music which makes glad the heart of God.

Unity in the Body

Mention has been made of the fact that in the latter half of Ephesians Paul dealt with God's election of a people to propagate his elected plan of salvation. In so doing he pled for unity in the body of Christ (4:1–16). In verse 1 he begged that each Christian would "walk worthy of the vocation [calling] wherewith ye are called." The Greek word rendered "worthy" has in it the idea of scales. Our manner of life should weigh as much as our calling from God.

Paul then told how this should be done "in love" as we "keep the unity of the Spirit in the bond of peace" (vv. 2–3). In verses 4–7 he used "one" seven times. "One body . . . one Spirit . . . one hope of your calling; one Lord [Jesus], one faith, one baptism [*baptisma,* denoting the meaning of baptism: death, burial, resurrection], one God and Father of all, who is above all, and through all, and in all" (vv. 4–6).

After describing the triumphant entry of Christ into heaven, Paul noted that he "gave gifts to men" (vv. 8,11). [6] These *gifts* were leaders in various areas of church life. Unfortunately the King James Version of verse 12 reads as if these were the duties to be performed by the *clergy*. Since the Greek text has no punctuation marks, the translators punctuated it as they understood it. This reflects the Church of England's polity where the clergy did the spiritual work, with little or no involvement of the laity. But Paul's meaning is that these leaders were to enlist and develop the laity for their role of service. Thus it may read: "For the purpose of equipping the saints [all Christians] with respect to the work of ministry, looking toward the goal of building up the body of Christ." This is in keeping with the New Testament principle of equal rights and responsibilities in the church. Verses 13–16 express the desired result: maturing the saints, resulting in unity in the faith, a full knowledge and spiritual stature of Christ—so that the body may be commensurate with Christ, who is the head of the church.

This goal involves every believer, every church, every denomination, and the cooperative unity of all. This is the goal of the New Testament and should be that of all believers.

Interchurch Relationships

This treatment would be incomplete without a brief look at the New Testament pattern of cooperation among local, democratic church bodies. That the churches in the New Testament were local autonomous bodies under the lordship of Christ is quite clear. At the same time there is the pattern of voluntary cooperation between churches in matters of mutual interest and concern. The two principal examples of this are cooperation between the churches in Antioch and Jerusalem in matters of doctrine (Acts 15; Gal. 2) and the offering taken by churches in Macedonia and Greece for the relief of needy Christians in Jerusalem (2 Cor. 8—9). In both cases cooperation was voluntary on the part of the churches involved.

This New Testament pattern is followed by Baptists in their denominational life. They cooperate through a loosely knit framework of local churches, district associations, state conventions, national conventions, and the Baptist World Alliance. Yet there is no organic union of any of these bodies. They are completely autonomous. No local church exercises authority over any other local church or denominational body. And no denominational body issues a mandate to any local church or other denominational body. Actions taken by any one of these are not binding upon any other body.

Local Southern Baptist churches do not send *delegates* to denominational meetings with delegated authority to act for them, in which case the actions of the body would be binding upon the churches. Instead, they send *messengers,* who comprise the given body. No action taken by them is binding upon any other body. Cooperation is purely voluntary right down to the individual member. Thus the right of equality is preserved for Baptist bodies as well as for individuals within the churches.

Following my election to the presidency of the Southern Baptist Convention, I was interviewed on a national radio network. The interviewer asked if I was the head of the Convention. Replying that I had been elected to its highest elective office, I added that Southern Baptists have no human *head.* He commented, "Then you are the head of a headless denomination." To which I responded, "Yes. That means I am a nobody." Asked about authority, I told him I had less than any one messenger. As a messenger I could make motions, debate issues, and vote. But as president I could only preside, having no vote unless there was a tie vote—which is practically nonexistent in a deliberative Baptist body.

So the principle of equal rights runs throughout the denominational bodies. A messenger from the smallest church represented in the Convention has the same rights as those from the largest church. The number of messengers from individual churches ranges from one to ten, ten being the maximum number allowed from even the largest churches. So no one church or group of churches can dominate. Issues are decided by the will of the majority, not by the will of a few. No one person speaks for Baptists. They speak for themselves, whether they do so in the local church or in any denominational body.

Sometimes this leads to rather stormy sessions. Many years ago I sat through a long afternoon session of the Southern Baptist Convention. It was filled with much debate as various positions were expressed. After the session I saw a newspaper with a boxcar-letter headline: *BAPTISTS TO DIVIDE!* I bought a copy to learn what they knew that I did not know. As I read it I found only an account of the afternoon's proceedings. Baptists were not about to divide. They were simply carrying on their business in a democratic process.

Yet with this loose relationship among the various bodies, Southern

Baptist churches received in 1976 one and one-half billion dollars for local and missionary causes. Millions of dollars were given for missions, ranging all the way from local missions to the uttermost parts of the earth. This is made possible not through coercion of one body upon another or of the local church upon anyone in its fellowship. The only *pressure* felt is that of personal conviction to cooperate as parts of Christ's body in furthering his cause in our Jerusalem, Judea, Samaria, and unto the ends of the earth. *Baptists are an independent people who express their independence through voluntary cooperation.*

Baptists have their differences concerning many things. But they are held together in voluntary unity through their faith in the Bible, the lordship of Christ, and the gigantic task of evangelism and missions. *Unity in diversity* is their secret. If you try to force them into a creedal mold, they will rebel. But challenge them to a world mission for Christ, and their diversities are sublimated to the call of a great task. J. B. Gambrell, a great commoner among Baptists a generation ago, once said that you cannot get many men excited about helping to kill a mouse, but you can enlist many to go on a bear hunt. Baptists are like that.

Many years ago when P. I. Lipsey was editor of the Mississippi *Baptist Record,* he rode a train from Jackson, Mississippi, to New Orleans, Louisiana. His seatmate was a Roman Catholic priest. Dr. Lipsey identified himself as a Baptist preacher. This led to quite a discussion of religion. Finally the priest asked, "Who is the head of the Southern Baptist Convention?" Asked what he meant by "head," he replied, "I mean someone like our pope." Dr. Lipsey said, "We have no such head." The priest said, "Well, the Lord help you!" and editor Lispey replied, "He is the one who does."

In this one simple answer lies the dual fact of every man's right to direct access to God and the right of all believers to equal privileges in the church.

Notes

[1] D. Miall Edwards, "Ordain," *The International Standard Bible Encyclopaedia* 4 (Grand Rapids: William B. Eerdmans, 1949), pp. 2199–2200.

[2] Baker, pp. 36–37, 51.

[3] Vedder, p. 397.

[4] G. Campbell Morgan, *The Gospel According to Matthew* (New York: Fleming H. Revell Company, 1929), p. 211.

[5] Hobbs, p. 74.

[6] When rulers and generals made triumphant entries, they threw money into the cheering throngs. But Christ gave his gifts to his people on earth.

7 / The Moral Axiom

To Be Responsible the Soul Must Be Free

This axiom is the basis of all ethics. Whether a person is ethical or unethical, the fact stems from his freedom to determine his conduct. Also, it speaks of man's very being. He is not a chance combination of atoms and molecules. While heredity and environment have roles in shaping one's character, he is not a prisoner to either. He is not a fated victim of preset chromosomes or of a crime-laden atmosphere. By diligent effort and willpower a person is able to rise above his forebears.

We have already noted that the sovereign God respects man's freedom. He knows that the will cannot be *forced*. A tyrant may put his foot upon a man's neck, but he cannot do so to his will. He may force a person's body to do wrong, but that person does not personally yield his will to evil except by his own free choice.

Whatever speculative philosophy or metaphysics may say about man, the spirit remains free. It may not be able to defend its freedom in a speculative or metaphysical way. But in its self-consciousness the soul shuts itself in its castle, closes the drawbridge and every other avenue of entrance, and defies the foe. It knows there is something wrong with any metaphysics which denies freedom; if metaphysics cannot overcome the difficulty, it is merely bad for metaphysics.

Our consciousness of freedom repudiates materialism. When materialism asserts that moral choices are the combinations of atoms and molecules in the dim past, the soul denies it. When a Christian gives a cup of cold water to another in the name of Christ or spends his life as a spiritual hero in the effort to redeem the islands of the sea, and materialists tell him his entire conduct was predestined by the dancing atoms before chaos had become cosmos, the Christian enters his quiet but nonetheless emphatic denial and passes on.

On the other hand, Christians deny the claim of materialism that moral values are relative, that the Ten Commandments are subject to change according to changing morés from generation to generation. If a luminous object holds its place in the firmament for thousands of years and is observed by the entire human race except a few men with defective vision, surely we are warranted in asserting that it is a fixed star and not a meteor. So it is that whether a person's actions be good or bad, whether he reacts positively or negatively in a given situation, we can insist that the key factor rests in his freedom of choice and not in the circumstances themselves.

The apostle Paul demonstrated his spirit of freedom as during his first Roman imprisonment he wrote Philippians with joy as its theme.

The opposite of Paul is Judas Iscariot. In circumstances of greedy frustration he betrayed Jesus. On the one hand Paul sang his way into the hall of fame of the ages. On the other Judas betrayed his way into the hall of infamy.

Freedom Inherent in Man's Nature

We have noted that man is the crown of God's creative work. Henry Giles reminds us that "man is greater than a world—than systems of worlds: there is more mystery in the union of soul with body than in the creation of a universe."

But no statement about man and his nature is so beautiful and striking as the simple words of Scripture. "And God said, Let us make man in our image, after our likeness" (Gen. 1:26). "Image" and "likeness" express the same idea—not a physical reproduction but one of nature and spirit. God did not create man as a puppet dangling from a cosmic string of fate. He made him a person, a self-conscious, reasoning person. And the appeal of the moral axiom is to man's personhood, his self-consciousness.

To be a person, man must be free. Thus God made him with the right of choice. He is free to choose but is responsible for his choices. He can as a finite being say yes or no even to the infinite God. This is evident in his first confrontation with temptation. Though in a state of innocence, he had to choose between God's will and Satan's will—between being righteous or unrighteous. And having chosen, he suffered the consequences of his tragic choice (Gen. 3:16–24).

God had made known his will (Gen. 2:15–17). In accepting the serpent's denial of the word and goodness of God, Eve rejected God's word—and Adam with her (Gen. 3:6). Thus we see the first sin that resulted from our primeval parents' abuse of the freedom God had given them.

Man does not like the word *sin*. Philosophy calls it an upward stumbling in the progress of the race. Biology explains it as a glandular disturbance. Psychology speaks of it as a maladjustment. Sociology relates it to environment. The Bible denies all of these. Sin is not an upward stumbling in progress but a downward falling in defeat. Adam and Eve had no glandular disturbance, but evil produces illness and death. In a state of innocence there could be no maladjustment. And the first sin was committed not in a *slum* but in a *paradise*.

The possibility of sin lay in man's being a person with the right of choice. Otherwise we make God the cause of man's sin, which is unthinkable. The first game of "passing the buck" was played in the garden of Eden. Adam sought to place the blame upon his associate—Eve. Ultimately he placed the blame upon God because of "the woman whom thou gavest to be with me" (Gen. 3:12). Adam was the first—but not the last—to try to blame sin upon *society*. But the biblical record denies such. Each person involved made a personal choice, had personal guilt and personal punishment.

Because of this abuse of freedom the fellowship between God and man was broken. A loving God resolved to restore it. But he did not do it by a divine fiat. Such a method would have destroyed man as a person. Instead, God began the long, difficult process that ultimately led to a cross and an empty tomb. God respected man's freedom. No gardener with a passionate love for growing things ever dealt so gently and skillfully with a delicate vine in training it to climb its trellis as God deals with the human will. But despite all that God has done for man's salvation and redemption of life, man still has the awesome power to say yes or no to God.

This granting of freedom to man is not an evidence of weakness in

God but of strength. An absolute dictatorship shows its weakness in denying any freedom to its subjects. Liberty granted to its subjects is evidence of democracy's strength.

God is not in the business of building robots, but of developing self-conscious and responsible human beings. A benevolent God is willing to face the possibility of man's failure, but he presents the opportunity for achievement to all.

Violation of Individual Freedom

Little needs to be said at this point, since violation of individual freedom has been covered in previous chapters. However, it is necessary to point out that any system of religion that attempts to stand between a person and God violates this precious right of persons made in God's image.

The Roman Catholic system is the direct antithesis of individual freedom. And any other system of Christianity which represents to any degree a diluted form of its practices to that extent violates human freedom. Beginning with infant baptism where parents and priest act for the child, the system evolves into an authoritative practice in which the church and its hierarchy stand between the individual soul and its direct responsibility to God. In the final analysis this is to treat one as a *thing* rather than as a *person* made in God's image.

One Monday following Easter I heard a mother, a Roman Catholic, describe to another the baptism of her infant the previous day. "Oh," she said, "how he kicked and cried! But the poor little thing did not understand what was happening to him."

Had he really known, he would have kicked and cried all the more. This was the first step in depriving him of his greatest dignity—the right of free choice in his relation to God. Through its authoritative priesthood, rites and rituals, and sacraments, including extreme unction, the Church had fastened its iron grip upon that soul, a grip that began with birth and does not end even in death. For through its unscriptural purgatory the soul is dependent upon priestly prayers to pass from there into heaven.

This is the worst of all tyrannies. And it is made worse by its claim to be in the name of God who made man free!

Freedom and Law

The Ten Commandments are the basis of the Mosaic code. The first four deal with man's relation to God; the last six relate to man's relation to other people. Thus they form the proper basis for all of life. Indeed, they express the moral and spiritual basis of the universe. They are not true because they are written in the Bible. They are in the Bible because they are eternally true.

A permissive psychology objects to the negative nature of all but two of the Commandments. However, these are not negations of selfish tyranny. They are expressions of infinite love. A wise, loving parent out of greater wisdom and experience should deny harmful things to children. Failure to do this is not an expression of love but of irresponsibility—indeed of a lack of true love. When needed discipline or helpful guidance is not given, that involves the selfish attitude of not wanting to be bothered. God is not like that. He is concerned for the welfare of every person. He knows that to do certain things or fail to do others brings dire consequences. So his moral and spiritual laws are designed to prevent such.

God is a God of law—whether it be in the natural, physical, moral, or spiritual realm. His laws are designed for benevolence toward all who live in accord with them. It is only when we live contrary to them that they take their toll in punishment. Let us suppose that a man defies the law of gravity by leaping from atop a skyscraper. God does not repeal that law to save him from his rash act. To do so would destroy the earth and all other people. The same holds true of all other law. Ignore physical law designed for health and life. The fruit is illness or death. Moral defiance produces moral corruption. Spiritual defiance brings spiritual death or eternal separation from God.

"Be not deceived; God is not mocked: for whatsoever a man soweth, that shall he also reap" (Gal. 6:7). In essence this means that you cannot turn up your nose at God and get away with it.

God has set his laws; he has taught them to man; but he does not coerce man into obeying them. Neither does he ignore the penalty for disobedience. This is not a punishment meted out arbitrarily by God. It is his law in operation. Man does not *break* but *violates* or lives contrary to God's laws. The laws go right on working and thus take their toll. This is the sense of God's wrath in Romans 1:18. It is not an emotion of God, but his benevolent law taking its toll upon those who live contrary to it. Man is free to choose to live by or contrary to them. But he is responsible for bearing the consequences of the latter attitude.

The Mosaic law and the Mosaic covenant (Ex. 19:1–6) are interrelated. We have noted that the covenant was one of law and service as noted in the "if" and "then" of verse 5. Until Israel kept the condition of the "if," God was not bound by the promise of the "then." In her freedom Israel accepted the conditions of the covenant (Ex. 19:8). Her subsequent history reveals a repeated rebellion against the covenant. This was also an expression of man's freedom—to be exact, an abuse of it. Through the centuries God did not drive Israel to obey the covenant. Rather, through his messengers he sought to draw her to honor it. "The Lord hath appeared of old unto me, saying, I have loved thee with an everlasting love: therefore with lovingkindness have I drawn thee" (Jer. 31:3; cf. Rom. 2:4).

The ultimate consequences of Israel's willful disobedience are seen in the Assyrian and Babylonian exiles. Seed sown by a free people bore a terrible harvest of captivity (cf. Hos. 8).

Thus we see how God deals with man's free will. He states his law. Living by it brings God's blessings. By his Spirit he seeks to lead man to live by it. Failure brings added visits of love mingled with warning. Only when man persists in rebellion does he finally reach the point of no return. Thus he leaves God no choice but to recognize such a state. And man is left to his fate.

After his scathing words to the Pharisees (Matt. 23) Jesus pronounced judgment upon the Jewish nation for its repeated rejection of him, a judgment that fell in A.D. 70. Matthew 23:38 reads, "Behold, your house is left unto you desolate." The last word is not in the Greek text. "Your house is left unto you." The nation chose to go it alone without God, so in its dire need it was left to itself. This illustrates the moral axiom in operation.

Jesus and Freedom

Jesus taught the moral freedom of man. More than this, he asserted it for himself. As a lad of twelve in the Temple he declared his prior allegiance to his Father; yet in Nazareth he willingly submitted to parental authority (Luke 2:46–51). In his wilderness temptations the Father did not coerce him, but helped him to decide what course his ministry would take (Matt. 4:1–11). The fact that he was *tempted* shows his freedom to yield to it or reject it. If he was not free to succumb to the devil's allurements, then they were not temptations. To deny this is to make him guilty of hypocrisy. Yes, he had the power to sin. But he also had the power not to sin. Insofar as his messiahship was concerned, like Adam and Eve, he was in a state of innocence—but with a disposition toward righteousness.

A comparison of Genesis 3:6 and the Gospel records of Matthew and Luke (4:1–13) shows that in both cases Satan tempted in three areas: physical appetite, aesthetic nature, and ambition. His every temptation still falls within these categories. Luke 4:13 speaks of "all [*panta* without the definite article, so "every single kind of"] the temptation." Hebrews 4:15 says that he "was in all points [again *panta* without the definite article] tempted like as we are, yet without sin." In Matthew 4:1 "to be tempted" is an infinitive of purpose. So God took the initiative to allow his Son in his free will to choose whether he would accept God's will or the devil's will. Satan succeeded with our primeval parents but failed with Jesus.

In all his intimate union with the Father there is never on the Father's part the slightest movement or impulse to override the voluntary choice of the Son. He came willingly into the world to work out God's eternal redemptive purpose (Heb. 10:5–7). In his sinless life he showed God *just* in his demand for righteousness in man. And having done so, he mounted the cross on man's behalf that in him God might be the justifier of all who believe in Jesus (Rom. 3:26). Knowing no sin experientially, he was made sin on our behalf that we might be made God's righteousness in him (2 Cor. 5:21).

In Gethsemane Jesus' struggle was not between him and Satan or between his will and the Father's will. It was a struggle within his own will, that he might do God's will whatever the cost. "My meat [the sustaining force in his life] is to do the will of him that sent me, and to finish his work" (John 4:34). His greatest crisis was in Gethsemane as the Father offered him the "cup" of being made sin. His sinless, sensitive soul drew back from so terrible a thing. But always his answer was, "O my Father, if this cup may not pass away from me, except I drink it, thy will be done" (Matt. 26:42). The supreme expression of his free will was that no one took his life from him; he laid it down of himself (John 10:18).

Christ and the Will

With respect to man it is the singular and special work of Christ to set free the individual will in such a manner that it unfolds in moral beauty in the personal character and coalesces socially with other wills in the beauty of a holy society.

The Anglo-Saxons made one chief contribution to the civilization of the world, the love of individual freedom. It has been asserted that this Anglo-Saxon sense of personality and love of freedom was found nowhere else. This perhaps is true insofar as the natural man is concerned.

However, in the deeper sense of the Spirit, this is exactly the gift that Christ bestows (John 8:32,36). The same love of freedom and sense of personality, the same self-assertion and love of adventure, the same response to challenge of danger and of great undertaking in a line of exact analogy to the old Anglo-Saxon principle—all this appears in Christianity, but with a vast difference. In Christ all is regenerated and spiritualized. Anglo-Saxon liberty was limited only by conditions of the physical environment—mountains, seas, and the stubborn moods of nature—and only these imposed a check upon its career. Christian liberty is limited only by the spiritual environment. But the inner impulse to personal and social development under Christ is like an endless spring fixed in the machinery of man's faculties and uncoiling itself through the centuries in ever-increasing vigor and power. Anglo-Saxon freedom without the Christian fire to purge and sanctify it leads to the superrace of Nietzsche, the finished product of which is seen in Nazism. It becomes a colossus of pitiless and selfish power and glories chiefly in the fact that it is destitute of love and the softer virtues.

Christian liberty, on the other hand, sends forth missionaries of love and mercy, bent not upon conquering the world but saving it. It builds hospitals, orphanages, and schools to minister in the name of Christ, to demonstrate in a tangible way the love of God in Christ Jesus. It follows the Holy Spirit in spiritual conquest as it storms the citadels of sin with a view toward bringing the kingdom of God in men's hearts, where righteousness should reign and where God who is love must hold sway. Christian freedom produces the moral and spiritual giants of history who, to the kingly elements of power, have added the priestly elements of love and service. God made us to be "kings and priests unto God."

The Gospel and Freedom

In no area of a person's life is freedom and responsibility more evident than in his response to the gospel message. Even before Jesus appeared on the public scene, his Forerunner sounded the note of personal responsibility before God. To the Pharisees and Sadducees John the Baptist said, "And think not to say within yourselves, We have Abraham to our father: for I say unto you, that God is able of these stones to raise up children unto Abraham" (Matt. 3:9). Thus he denied the idea of heredity as giving spiritual rights and privileges apart from personal choice and corresponding character. The Jews were not true sons of Abraham because they were simply physical descendants of Abraham. Heredity did not bind or negate the will, and it did not exempt the will from moral choices and personal obedience in the New Covenant.

Jesus' greatest difficulty with Nicodemus was at this very point (John 3:1–18). A person's own will is not involved in his physical birth. But to be born again or from above calls for a personal act of repentance from sin and faith in God's Son. In this encounter Jesus set the pattern for the gospel message through the ages. For while salvation is by grace, it becomes personal only through the willing choice of faith in Jesus on the part of the individual.

Freedom is self-determination. This does not mean that the will is without bias or that human choices are uninfluenced by external forces, by other human personalities, or by divine influences of grace. It only means that when a person acts he acts for himself. The choice is his own. He is not compelled but impelled. When all the above-mentioned forces have done their work, a person must retire into the privacy of his own soul and decide the issue. One will search in vain for the slightest hint of a proxy faith in the gospel.

Freedom is self-determination in every area of life. In civil life political freedom is self-government, even though one must act in terms of what is best for all. The individual is free politically only when he exercises his function as a citizen without artificial or unjust extraneous hindrance. One of the major difficulties when free nations try to negotiate with Communist nations is the difference of meaning in terms. Under Communism *peace* is the inability of another state to resist totalitarianism; *right* is that which furthers the cause of Communism; and *freedom* is nothing more than its people's freedom to submit. *Free elections* are a mockery when the voter has no choice but to approve the one candidate listed on the ballot. For a person to really be politically free he must have the right to choose.

To have intellectual freedom means to be intellectually self-determined. One's beliefs are not imposed by authority but accepted as his own free act. Industrial freedom is the privilege of self-determination in the economic world. Unjust discriminations, class legislation, and inequitable adjustments of the industrial machinery at any point, whether by captial or labor, impair or subvert industrial freedom. Invasion of privacy by government or by any other social group is to place a knife at the jugular vein of a free people.

In morals freedom is self-determination in conduct. In religion freedom is exemption from State compulsion, social coercion, ecclesiastical or priestly authority, creedal binding, or parental acts. Religious freedom on its positive side is God appealing to the soul through truth and calling forth the soul's intelligent and obedient response. It is the soul's approach to God through faith, prayer, and fellowship and obtaining grace to help in time of need.

Jesus never sought to use physical or political power to gain a favorable response to his message. He taught, loved, and called. But to everyone he preserved the right of that person to say yes or no. This is seen in his call to both salvation and service (John 1:37–51; Mark 1:17–20; cf. Matt. 11:28–30). He repeatedly refused the role of a political-military Messiah. And though he loved the rich young ruler in a special way, he did not use the pressure of his little finger to force belief upon him. The father of the prodigal son did not restrain him from leaving home. Neither did he go and force him to return. But his love reached out to him across the miles. And he joyfully welcomed his return.

Jesus said, "No man can come to me, except the Father which hath sent me draw him" (John 6:44). This does not mean that only a select few are drawn. It means that the Father in sending his Son has taken the initiative in redemption. That is God's part. "Come" is man's part as in the exercise of his free will he believes in Jesus as his personal Savior.

In Revelation 3:20 is the unforgettable scene of Christ standing at the door and knocking. Literally it reads: "I permanently stand at the door, and keep on knocking: if any man at any time may hear my voice, and open the door, I will come in [a definite promise] to him, and I will sup [have table fellowship] with him, and he with me." Christ stands and knocks. But each person must open the door. He will not come in by force. To do that would destroy human personhood.

On the negative side, there is no clearer picture of free choice and personal responsibility than in the case of Judas Iscariot. Why Jesus chose him as one of the twelve will ever remain a mystery. Perhaps, like the others, he possessed qualities which if surrendered to Jesus would have been of special value in the young Christian movement. But the overall evidence is that he never yielded himself to him. One year before his death Jesus took note of forces at work in Judas which ultimately would lead to his act of betrayal (John 6:70–71): "One of you *is* a devil." He was not one when Jesus chose him.

Judas never called Jesus "Lord." To him he was only "Master" —rabbi or Teacher. In Matthew 26:22 the others called Jesus "Lord." But Judas called him "Master" (v. 25; cf. v. 49). He was never a believer in Jesus for who and what he was. If there were any instance in which the Lord would have brought pressure to bear, it seems that it would have been upon this member of the most intimate circle. But his only pressure was his compelling love. But he did not force his will. For this reason Judas' betrayal is all the more terrible.

Varied sentimental efforts have been made to absolve Judas from guilt. Some would make him a superpatriot—he betrayed Jesus to prevent a revolution against Rome which would have destroyed the Jewish nation. Others portray him as a super-Christian—they say that he sought by drastic means to force Jesus to declare his messiahship. And, of course, there are those who see Judas as God's chosen instrument to make possible the crucifixion of his Son. This is contrary to the very nature of God and his respect for human personality.

Now hear Jesus himself on this matter. "But, behold, the hand of him that betrayeth me is with me on the table. And truly the Son of man goeth, as it was determined: but woe unto that man by whom he is betrayed" (Luke 22:21–22). It is true that God willed that his Son die on a cross for the world's sin. But the characters involved in that black day were not mindless automatons with no will of their own. Judas was the betrayer but not by divine compulsion. Every word of Scripture about him belies this idea. With the same spiritual forces playing upon him which led the other apostles to believe in Jesus, he betrayed him. His dastardly deed effected God's redemptive purpose. But he did it in the free choice of his own will.

Paul and Freedom

Volumes could be written about the details of Paul's teachings about moral freedom and responsibility. But instead of examining these, let us look at the man himself. Brought up in an atmosphere of legalism, he found freedom in Christ through a conscious decision. This experience changed the entire course of his life.

A sense of power conjoined with freedom is characteristic of the best Christians—of those who choose Christ for themselves and make him their ideal. Nowhere do you find such spontaneity and grandeur, such untrammeled energy and buoyancy as in Christians. The prime example is Paul.

He abounds in images that suggest spontaneity and exuberant joy.
See him yonder when like a mighty swimmer, he rises above the billows
of adversity and difficulty, and exclaims, "I can do all things through
Christ" (Phil. 4:13). Hear him as he spreads the wings of devotion, and
in a splendid flight of mystic passion shouts, "For to me to live is
Christ, and to die is gain" (Phil. 1:21). Observe him as he is caught in
the mighty grip of moral enthusiasm and self-conquest, exulting in the
joy of battle: "Thanks be unto God, who always causeth us to triumph
in Christ" (2 Cor. 2:14). See him again as he is impelled onward, the
embodiment of flaming love and quenchless hope, and deathless ambition, running the Christian race as one who treads the air, and exclaim-
ing, "Forgetting those things which are behind . . . I press toward the
mark for the prize of the high calling of God in Christ Jesus" (Phil.
3:13–14). The fact that these quoted sayings are from 2 Corinthians
written following a major crisis in the Corinthian church and from
Philippians, dictated while Paul was chained to a Roman prison guard,
makes them all the more meaningful. But they are typical of the
indomitable spirit of the great apostle.

The moral career of Paul reminds one of the flight of some mighty
eagle long confined to a cage and then released; at first he is uncertain of
his new feeling of freedom, but at length, becoming conscious of it the
heavy eyelids open, he looks about him, his drooping wings he gathers
for flight and then, with a scream of joy, he soars away to the clouds
where he "bathes his plumage in the thunder's home." His eagle soul
has found its object in God's free air. Jesus Christ is the atmosphere of
the soul.

And this is the secret of Christ's authority over men. Through him
they find themselves. It is a paradox, but it is forever true. Men are the
slaves of Christ because he makes them free to be themselves—in him.

Freedom and License

With free men there is no greater problem than how to use freedom.
The abuse of freedom may empty it of its meaning or even destroy it
altogether. Totalitarian government is the final bitter residue of freedom

in the political sphere that has been prostituted as license.

In the spiritual sphere men outside of Christ are slaves to sin. Jesus said, "And ye shall know the truth, and the truth shall make you free . . . . Whosoever committeth [having the habit of doing] sin is the servant [slave] of sin . . . . If the Son therefore shall make you free [liberate you], ye shall be free indeed" (John 8:32,34,36). Even so, each person's will is involved in this freedom, both in receiving Jesus and in the commitment of his life to him.

A man said to a pastor, "I wish I could believe in salvation by grace through faith, and that once saved I could never be lost again. If I did, then I would get saved and have the time of my life doing what I want to do." The pastor replied, "Yes, you would have the time of your life doing what you want to do. But if you really get saved, the things you would want to do are quite different from what you are now thinking about."

Of course, this depends upon what we mean by salvation. Too often we think of it as a fire insurance policy for the soul. It is much more than that. Salvation involves regeneration, sanctification, and glorification: respectively, the saving of the soul, the saving of the dedicated Christian life, and the sum total of glory and reward in heaven, including the resurrection of the body.

Charles Kingsley once said, "There are two freedoms—the false, where a man is free to do what he likes; the true, where a man is free to do what he ought." Paul faced this matter in 1 Corinthians 8 (cf. Rom. 14). The issue was whether a Christian should eat meat offered the idols. Pagans saw this as part of their worship. But meat used in worship was often sold for public consumption. Certain weak Christians did not distinguish between the pagan practice and simply eating this meat for food. In their Christian freedom "strong" Christians distinguished between the two. Paul identified himself with the strong (vv. 4,8). But for him and others to eat this meat violated the consciences of the weak. So Paul warned the strong against becoming a stumbling block to the weak. The latter might be led to eat this meat contrary to their convictions, and to them it would be a sin (vv. 10–12). Although he had every right to eat this meat, Paul concluded, "Wherefore, if meat make my brother to offend [stumble], I will eat no flesh while the world standeth [unto the age, forever], lest it make my brother to offend [stumble]'' (v. 13).

It is better to forego some rights if they are harmful to others. Things that may not be sinful in themselves become sins of wrong influence if they cause others to stumble. Freedom to choose is also freedom to choose not to do some things which hurt others.

In 1 Corinthians 2:14 to 3:1 Paul spoke of three kinds of men: natural, carnal, and spiritual. The natural man is the unregenerated man. The carnal man is a Christian who is still controlled by his fleshly desires. The spiritual man is the Spirit-controlled man. At regeneration one becomes a babe in Christ. It is God's will that one will grow into an adult (a perfect or complete man, Eph. 4:13) in Christ. As in the physical life, so in the spiritual life—this adult goal is not achieved in a day. Simultaneously with regeneration the believer is sanctified or set apart to God's service (note ''saints''' or sanctified ones in 1 Cor. 1:2; 2 Cor. 1:1). But he must grow in that state as he progresses toward the goal which is Christ.

In Galatians 5:13 Paul warned against abusing Christian freedom by making it ''an occasion to the flesh.'' In a larger degree he treated this matter in Romans 6. Salvation is by grace through faith, but grace makes its demands. Whereas once we were slaves to sin and used our bodies to serve the devil, now as Christians we should become slaves to Christ and serve him with the same dedication (vv. 1,14–19). In Romans 7 he dealt with the civil war which raged in his body. Some see verses 7–25 as referring to Paul's pre-Christian experience. I see this to be true of verses 7–13. But the predominant use of the present tense in verses 14–25 leads me to see this as related to Paul's struggle after he became a Christian. His only hope is to yield himself fully to Christ through the Holy Spirit. If Paul had this struggle, certainly no other Christian can expect to escape it.

The point is that once one chooses Christ as Savior, the struggle with sin is not finished. It enters a new dimension. When the devil loses your soul to Christ, he then endeavors to destroy the joy and usefulness of your Christian life. In 1 Corinthians 3:11–15 Paul showed the tragedy of such a life. It is not a question of a lost regeneration but of a loss in fruitfulness for Christ. Thus the moral axiom of freedom and responsibility runs throughout the Christian life.

Freedom and Eschatology

Indeed, our dignity of free choice reaches even beyond this life. If by one's own choice he rejects Christ as Savior, he alone is responsible for being in hell for eternity. But even there the Bible teaches degrees of punishment (Luke 12:47–48). Paul said that both Jew and Gentile (pagan) who reject Christ will be judged by the degree of opportunity against which each sins (Rom. 2:11–16). It is proper to be concerned about the heathen who never hear the gospel. But in light of degrees of punishment in hell, we should be even more concerned about the man in a community filled with churches who regularly hears the gospel and yet never chooses Christ as Savior.

Furthermore, the Bible teaches degrees of reward in heaven (Matt. 25:14–23; Luke 19:12–19). All who receive Christ will be there. And each will enjoy heaven to the extent of his ability, but the ability of one will be greater than that of another as determined by how he lived his Christian life on earth. The final judgment will not determine who will be saved or lost. It will only declare it. All whose names are in "the book of life" will be in heaven. All others will be in hell (Rev. 20:15). According to Luke 16:19–26 the saved and lost at death go immediately to heaven or hell (cf. 2 Cor. 5:1–8).

The judgment will be out of "the books" (Rev. 20:12). "They were judged every man according to their works" (v. 13). This is why the final judgment of each person comes at the end of the age rather than immediately following death (Rom. 14:10,12). "For we must all appear before the judgment seat of Christ; that every one may receive the things done in his body, according to that he hath done, whether it be good or bad" (2 Cor. 5:10). A righteous judgment cannot be rendered until all the evidence is in. That will be true only at the end of the age, when the full fruits of our deeds, good or bad, will be revealed.

So the choices we make have eternal import. They are not merely for the moment and then forgotten. They set in motion forces for good or evil that may result in many persons being saved or lost before the Lord returns. This is why even a cup of water given in the Lord's name yields such great reward—not on the basis of the water's value, but on that of its spiritual results. By the same token, what we consider small sins are just as harmful to the way others look at us and the way we feel about ourselves as other, "more serious" sins.

Yes, we are free to receive Christ or to reject him. But we are responsible for our choice. We are free to live or not to live a full Christian life. But we are also responsible for the life we live. Therefore, we should be careful how we use this awesome right of choice. For we shall meet it at the end of the age—and must live with it in eternity.

8 / The Religio-Civic Axiom

A Free Church in a Free State

Should someone feel that some of the axioms treated thus far are largely academic in nature, no one familiar with the modern scene can so regard this one. It is headline news. That for which our forefathers fought, suffered, and died is in dire peril today. And, sad to say, in some cases it has suffered at the hands of its friends. Since we have already treated the struggle for religious liberty that involves the separation of church and state, it is not necessary to repeat it here. It should be recalled, however, that the papacy has never relinquished its claim to authority over both church and state. And some European countries still have established churches. Dissenters pay taxes to support a state church whose teachings and practices are contrary to their faith. In such countries there is religious toleration, but that is a far cry from religious liberty.

In his famous sermon on Baptists and religious liberty delivered from the Capitol steps in Washington, George W. Truett said, "There is a vast difference between toleration and liberty. Toleration is a concession; liberty is a right; toleration is a matter of expediency; liberty is a matter of principle; toleration is a grant of man; liberty is a gift of God."

Separation a Principle

The concept of the separation of church and state is based more on principle than on proof texts. To be sure, Jesus' words "Render therefore unto Caesar the things which are Caesar's; and unto God the things that are God's" (Matt. 22:21) constitute a clear statement of the principle. The record makes clear that the early Christians were good citizens in things pertaining to Caesar (Rom. 13:1–10; 1 Pet. 2:12–17). Even some early Roman writers testify to this fact. Only when Caesar tried to claim for himself the position of God did Christians refuse to obey. The record of Roman persecution of Christians is too well known to require further word here.

Though the Sanhedrin was primarily a religious body among the Jews, it functioned in certain civic affairs also. The refusal of Peter and John to stop preaching about Jesus Christ also involves this principle of separation (Acts 4:18–20). God had spoken to these apostles. And his mandate was of such nature that the word of man could not gainsay it or defeat it. While they defied the Sanhedrin, they were ready to suffer the human consequences of doing so. But at the same time they had the witness in their hearts that they were pleasing to God. Peter expressed his attitude in 1 Peter. If suffer they must they would not do so as evildoers or criminals but as Christians (4:15–16). As the first Christians to suffer bodily for Christ following the Lord's ascension, they head the long line of such down the centuries. All have in deeds if not in words repeated these noble and heroic words of the apostles: "Whether it be right in the sight of God to hearken unto you more than unto God, judge ye. For we cannot but speak the things which we have seen and heard" (Acts 4:19–20). Persecutions reflected in New Testament books such as 1 Peter and Revelation reveal the principle that no outside authority, civil or religious, should come between the soul and God.

But back of all these is the principle of the competency of the soul in religion, one expression of which is the right of direct access to God. It is evident also in the right of free choice, which is an integral part of man's nature. No one can surrender these principles or encroach upon them without living counter to the Scriptures and violating the will of God.

Violation of This Principle

In the Roman Empire the religions of conquered peoples were declared legal religions when their gods were placed in the Pantheon in Rome. Since Judaism had no images of God, it was declared a legal religion without his *image* being placed in the Pantheon. At the outset Christianity was regarded as simply one branch of Judaism. But when it became evident that this was not the case, Christianity became an illegal religion. The decision of Gallio in Corinth about A.D. 51 which favored Paul over the Jews was perhaps the first step toward giving Christianity a legal status (Acts 18:12–16). But many years of persecution by the Roman state lay ahead.

The first persecution of Christians as a policy of the state came under Nero, who reigned A.D. 54–68. He burned the city of Rome with a view to rebuilding it as a beautiful city. When the populace rose up about it, he blamed it on the Christians. In a severe but somewhat localized persecution he made them the scapegoat.

The second persecution was under Domitian (A.D. 81–96). It centered in the Christians' refusal to worship him as a god and to agree that "Caesar is Lord." Instead they said, "Jesus is Lord." Since Caesar was identified with the state, this was regarded as lack of loyalty to the empire. Persecution continued under various emperors, but none was so severe as that under Domitian.

Christians probably breathed a sigh of relief when in 313 Constantine, the western emperor, and the eastern emperor Licinius issued the Edict of Milan, which granted full toleration to Christianity. [1] During a crucial battle with Maxentius in 312, Constantine claimed that he had seen a vision in the heavens which gave his victory. This led him to adopt Christianity. However, Constantine's purpose was political in nature. He saw Christianity as a unifying force that could hold together a crumbling empire. He continued to support pagan religions, even retaining the title of chief priest in their system. The remainder of his life does not depict Christian virtues. In the belief that baptism washed away sins, he delayed receiving this rite until he was at the point of death. Theodosius (378–395) was the first emperor to declare Christianity as the state religion. [2]

What may have appeared to be a blessing at the time proved in the long run to be a curse. Being a state religion robbed Christianity of its independence. Succeeding centuries showed that it sapped its vitality. It opened the floodgates to a tide of unregenerated people coming into the church. And it ushered in centuries of struggle for supremacy between the church and the state. Religious wars, massacres, and persecutions have blighted history's pages in the name of Christ! Such could have been avoided if our axiom had been followed—that the state has no authority in the religious opinions and practices of men, and the church has no right to dictate to the state.

One cannot avoid noting that the first coalition of church and state in Christian history nailed Jesus to a cross. Institutional religion judged him worthy of death and pressured institutional government to carry out its verdict. This set the pattern for later persecution of Christians by the church and its use of the arm of government to do its bloody work.

For many centuries the struggle between church and state was an unequal one. By a sort of spiritual instinct the church tugged at her chains with various movements of protest against the English and European establishments. At this time Roger Williams founded the colony of Rhode Island. Through that break in the dark clouds of oppression beamed a tiny ray of religious liberty. Man had entered into a new era of religious liberty.

Meaning of the First Amendment

We have seen that this First Amendment to the United States Constitution was in great measure the fruit of constant Baptist insistence. Their view of soul freedom and separation of church and state is seen in their earliest known confessions of faith, and their practice as a denomination has never parted company with their doctrine. There has never been a time in their history, so far as that history is known to us, when as a corporate people they wavered in their doctrine of a free church in a free state. Even those who, through their misguided zeal for a particular cause, have placed this principle in jeopardy hold tenaciously to this principle.

The portion of the First Amendment related to this study reads, "Congress shall make no law respecting an establishment of religion, or prohibiting the free exercise thereof." One thing is quite clear. This amendment prohibits an *established* church in the United States. No religious group is to be designated as the state church, such as the Anglicans in England and the Presbyterians in Scotland. The citizenry will not be taxed for the purpose of supporting any religious faith, even one with which many do or do not agree. Even though there may be but

one system of faith in the nation, it may not be established and supported by tax money—federal, state, or local.

This amendment also forbids laws that prohibit the free exercise of
religion, whether it be Christianity, Judaism, Islam, Buddhism,
animism, or whatever. No person can be forced by law to espouse any
religion or to profess faith in deity. This amendment recognizes the
competency of the soul in religion, the right of direct access to God, and
the freedom of choice with respect to religion. Here, then, is religious
freedom, not religious toleration. As one has said, "It is an accepted
axiom by all Americans that the civil power ought to be not only neutral
and impartial as between entirely different forms of faith, but ought to
leave these matters on one side, regarding them no more than they
regard the artistic or literary pursuits of its citizens."

In short, the entire contents of the axiom are summed up in the
statement that the state has no ecclesiastical function and the church no
civic function. The First Amendment, which expresses the heart of this
axiom, says that the state should not control the church and the church
should not control the state. It was born out of the bitter experience of
Europe where first one and then the other of these bodies sought to
control or did control the other.

Baptists along with others heartily agree that the state should not
control the church. But strangely, even many Baptists are not adamantly
against the church controlling the state. Some years ago I was asked to
speak on the separation of church and state at a statewide gathering of
Baptist pastors. My statement that the state should not try to tell
churches how to run their business was greeted with enthusiastic amens.
But a strange silence ensued when I said that the church should not try to
tell the state how to run its affairs. This was a most eloquent silence.

As Christian citizens we should exert our influence in the interest of
good government. But no corporate segment of the church should
deliver mandates to any area of civil government. Under the First
Amendment they have the right "to petition the Government for a
redress of grievances." But this is a far cry from a mandate. Our axiom
calls for a free church in a free state. Neither should be subservient to
the other.

It should be noted, however, that the principle of separation is not always easy to interpret. It is one thing to state certain principles involved, but it is quite another to interpret the gray areas that lie between the two extremes. Through the years some of the most brilliant legal minds in the nation have struggled with exact interpretations in this area.

Take, for instance, the matter of using tax money for the support of parochial schools. Quite plainly the First Amendment forbids the government to prohibit the operation of such schools. It can require that they have certain academic standards if their graduates are to be accepted in state schools of higher learning. However, the various accrediting groups take care of this matter, thus making unnecessary any governmental interference. With public schools turning out some graduates who are unable to read and write to the extent that they cannot even fill out job applications, it would seem that the various levels of government should begin by looking to their own standards.

But what about the matter of tax money being used in any degree to support schools, one of whose reasons for being is to include in its curriculum the teaching of one particular religion or faith? It is a matter of record that Roman Catholics are the greatest agitators to this end. If they fail at one point of attack they shift to another. Their churches have no Sunday Schools or other like programs, using their parochial schools instead to teach their particular faith.

It is argued by some that it is the state's responsibility to educate its people. Very well! Let them attend public schools provided for that purpose. Some insist that they are taxed to support public schools and then must pay the costs of sending their children to parochial schools— so double taxation. The government does not require that these children attend the latter. So it is a parental choice, not legal coercion, which produces this situation. If the school system provides a bus for children to ride to school, but some parents prefer that theirs ride in Cadillacs or Lincolns, should the government pay for the latter? Just because tax money is used to provide books, lunches, and transportation for public schools does not automatically mean that they should do the same for private schools.

When John F. Kennedy ran for president many Baptists and other evangelicals opposed his election simply because they feared that a Roman Catholic would fall short in the matter of the separation of church and state. To the delightful surprise of many, he stood firmly upon this principle even in the face of opposition from the leadership of his own faith. He did so far more than his non-Catholic predecessors had done. Nor did he appoint an envoy to the Vatican.

James E. Wood, Jr. of the Baptist Joint Committee on Public Affairs (which represents various Baptist bodies) spoke in keeping with the Baptist position when he said, "(1) The Vatican can communicate with the United States government in the way any religious group communicates with it; (2) The Vatican maintains an apostolic delegate in Washington in the manner of an ambassador; and (3) since Rome is at once the capital of Italy and location of the Vatican, the United States has an embassy in Rome already."

What about prayer in public schools? Perhaps no decision ever handed down by the United States Supreme Court produced more outcry than its decision on this matter. Unfortunately the first news report on this decision gave a wrong impression. The Court could have helped in the situation by clarifying its decision. One of the nine justices did deny that the ruling forbade all prayers in the public schools. But it was largely lost in the pandemonium of the time. Thus school administrators and attorneys general have appeared confused on the matter.

Exactly what was the point on which the Court ruled? The question was whether a government agency or employee could prepare a prayer and require that it be used in public schools. The ruling was that it was not constitutional according to the First Amendment. In speaking on this matter from the pulpit, I declared that I would balk if the deacons wrote out a prayer and required me to use it. The Supreme Court did not rule on the matter of *voluntary* prayer in public schools! That is another issue entirely. But from a total misunderstanding of the ruling we have seen frantic school administrators banning voluntary prayer, religious exercises, baccalaureate sermons, and Bible reading in many schools.

The majority decision in this ruling was prepared by Justice Hugo Black, a Baptist. It reads like a treatise on Baptist church history as it recalls religious persecution in Europe and the American colonies. It was against this background that the First Amendment was adopted and should be interpreted.

Speaking of the use of the Bible in public schools, here again many labor under a misapprehension. The role of the schools is to prepare young people for living a rich, productive, and well-rounded life. This certainly involves the teaching of history, culture, and moral values. The Bible may be read and taught for these purposes. But sectarian interpretation is something else.

Recently a Jewish rabbi said in my presence that in Israel's public schools the curriculum includes a study of the life of Jesus (he added, "Note that I said 'Jesus,' not 'Christ' "). This study is required as a part of Jewish culture and history.

By way of protest it should also be noted that if we are to consider Bible reading and prayer as a violation of the First Amendment, it should also be considered a violation when some teachers in both grade school and university level teach *against* the Bible, God, Christ, and other basics of the Judeo-Christian faith. Consistency is a rare jewel indeed!

Now having said these things we hasten to add that the primary responsibility in teaching and interpreting the Bible and in the development of devotional life lies upon the home and the church. We should not place solely upon the public schools a burden which, under God, the home and church should bear for themselves.

Relations Between Church and State

The First Amendment is not a wall which says absolutely that the church and the state have no relations or responsibilities with each other. They are both important elements in the social order, and as such they do have relationships one with the other.

Yet the functions of church and state are quite distinct. The church is a voluntary organization; the state compels obedience. One organization is spiritual; the other is temporal. The direct allegiance in the church is to God; in the state it is to law and government. The latter is for the protection of life and property; the former is for the promotion of spiritual life. As one has stated it, Christ is not to be brought before Caesar's judgment seat; neither is he to be placed upon Caesar's throne. The church is compatible with the state, but entirely independent of it.

The Christian bears two relations: one to God and the other to the earthly state in which he lives. Moffatt translates Philippians 3:20, "But we are a colony of heaven." The Revised Standard Version reads, "But our commonwealth is in heaven." The New American Standard Bible uses "citizenship" but footnotes "commonwealth." Moffatt's translation reflects the idea that Philippi was a Roman colony set down among a hostile, conquered people. It was a little bit of Rome in that location. Frank Stagg says, "The idea [commonwealth or citizenship] may have had a special appeal and meaning in a city like Philippi, a Roman colony. Although living in Macedonia, they were citizens of Rome with privileges and responsibilities of Romans (cf. 1:27)." [3]

Among the Roman privileges were exemption from certain taxes and the right of citizenship. Responsibilities involved keeping the peace, guarding the empire from invasion, and living as Romans so as to cause others to desire to be Romans. As a colony of heaven the Philippian church was a little bit of heaven located in a hostile world. Its privileges involved its relation to God. Among its responsibilities was the obligation to live as Christians, so as to lead others to want to become Christians. Certainly they were to be a law-abiding people where those laws did not conflict with their prior loyalty to God.

As for the relationship between the state and church, the state is to provide a proper atmosphere wherein the church can do its work. This is true with regard to other elements in the social order. The church is to produce people of Christian character, good citizens, through whose efforts and influence will result a peaceful, proper social order. From the churches' standpoint they are to be spiritual light and salt in the world (Matt. 5:13–16).

The state has no right to tax the churches; neither do the churches have the right to use tax funds to further their spiritual ministry. The right to tax is the right to control, even to destroy. God has provided that citizens should pay taxes to support government (Rom. 13:6–7). He has ordained tithes and offerings for the support of his spiritual works (Mal.

3:8–10). The state has no right to invade the latter for its support; the church has no right to accept or demand the former for its work.

There are those who insist that tax exemption of churches constitutes an establishment of religion. But this is no more true than it is that tax exemption for eleemosynary institutions means their establishment. The church enhances the value of all other property, adds to the desirability of any community as a place to live, builds up our civilization in many ways, and is the most efficient of all police forces. It is thus a quid pro quo to the state and more than earns its exemption from taxation.

Many years ago a young preacher established a mission in the most juvenile crime-infested area of St. Louis. A year later the policeman on that beat expressed amazement at the tremendous decrease in the crime rate. That mission had saved the city and society far more than the few tax dollars involved in its exemption. Justified anxiety is felt throughout the nation about the high crime rate among juveniles. This situation is not confined to the underprivileged areas of society, but often includes children of affluent families. The solution to this problem lies not in more policemen, but in more discipline and moral teaching in the home. These alarming statistics could be greatly reduced if the homes and churches cooperated in the proper rearing and spiritual training of children.

By their very nature there are some things the state can do for the church and vice versa that neither can do for itself. For instance, the state provides fire and police protection for the churches. The churches are not billed for these services. On the other hand, suppose that the federal government needs someone to do certain scientific research, but has no one in its employment qualified to do it. However, there is a professor of science in a denominational college who is qualified. So the government gives the professor a grant for the project. The two institutions assist each other in accomplishing a good for the nation. Yet each maintains its freedom from the other. However, the professor should do the research on his time, not on that for which he is paid by the college.

More to the point is a project in which the writer was involved. During World War II, I was pastor in Alexandria, Louisiana, the most concentrated troop training area in the country. I was also chairman of the operating board for the local Baptist hospital. Thousands of wives of soldiers came there to be near their husbands as long as possible. While there hundreds of them gave birth to their babies.

One day the commanding general of the area came to our board with a request. The military had no hospital facilities in which to place these wives for their babies to be born. He said that even if he had a hospital he could spare no medical personnel to use it. So he asked if we would erect a maternity building on land we owned adjacent to our hospital. We said that we did not have the money with which to do it. He offered to let us have the money.

Immediately, we thought of the separation of church and state. At a called meeting of the Baptist state executive board we presented the matter. A committee was appointed to study it with power to act, since time was of the essence. I was made chairman of the committee. The committee faced a dilemma. Should we affirm this principle of separation and ignore a dire human need? All but one member agreed that we should cooperate with the military. But this one sincerely could not agree. He said, "I do not believe that we should accept one penny from the government. We should not use tax money for any church assistance."

Finally I asked him, "If your church building were on fire, would you call the fire department?" He replied, "Of course I would." "Then would you expect to pay for their service?" "Of course not," he said. I told him that our "house" was on fire. With that he agreed that we should proceed.

Here was a government with plenty of money, but no medical personnel. Here was a church-related hospital with no money, but with ample medical personnel. So we cooperated by pooling our resources. In drawing up the necessary papers the government's attorneys were as careful as we were to protect the principle of separation of church and state. We worked together as equals to meet the emergency of a dire human need.

In order to satisfy those Baptists who might not see the fine point in this gray area, the hospital kept separate records of this transaction. It entered the money received from the government as a *debit*. Whenever it treated any patient who was in any way related to the military—wives and children—it gave them a discounted rate. The amount of the discount was entered on the *credit* side. This was continued until the ledger balanced.

In neither case did the church or state violate the sovereignty of the other. We remained a free church in a free state cooperating to meet a common need.

Dangers to the Separation Principle

That these dangers exist cannot be denied by anyone cognizant with the modern scene. And they are a matter of great concern to those who cherish the principle of separation of church and state.

But before looking at these, let us examine another but similar matter which throws light on the matter. From its inception the public school system has largely been under local control. By "local" we refer to city, county, and state levels. It was also financed by the same. But about 1950 local school boards began looking to the federal government for money with which to finance the growing demand of public schools. Had local communities shown the courage to tax themselves for school needs, they could have used all the receipts at home. Instead, they turned to Washington for federal funds. The result was simply increased federal taxes, so that the local community sent one dollar to Washington and received back perhaps thirty-five cents. No money tree grows in Washington. The government's only source of more revenue is further taxation of the people. But the greater tragedy was not more taxes and a loss in ultimate revenue at the local level. It was the loss of the right of self-determination at the local school level. We would have done well to have heeded words of Benjamin Franklin. "They that give up essential liberty to obtain a little temporary safety deserve neither liberty nor safety."

Edmund Burke reminds us that "people never give up their liberties but under some delusion." In this case the delusion was people thinking they were getting something for nothing.

Sadly, in matters of major policy, local school boards are now at the mercy of federal judges and Washington bureaucrats, none of which is responsible to the electorate. In the power struggle between these and local school patrons the greatest sufferers are the children and the teachers. And in it all, standards of education have been ignored or lowered to the point of tragedy. Lawsuits are common in which parents sue school boards for improper education for their children. One cannot help wondering how these parents would have voted on an issue to increase local school taxes rather than going to Washington for a handout. This should serve as a warning to churches and church-related institutions. They should not succumb to the delusion of getting something for nothing.

No denomination should have more schools than it can/will support, for it cannot afford the luxury (?) of governmental grants of funds. It is still true that what the federal government finances it ultimately will control.

The editor of the Texas *Baptist Standard* (October 6, 1976) said, "Government control always follows government money. If Baptists can't [or won't] finance their colleges without tax funds it will be best for government and Baptists that Baptists get out of the school business."

A tragic story, dated August 19, 1976, concerned Western Maryland College, a Methodist institution which formerly had received that denomination's support. But in 1975 it received "$373,000 in unrestricted state and Federal funds," with a similar amount to come annually in the future. After three years of litigation of a charge by the Maryland affiliate of the American Civil Liberties Union and Americans United for Separation of Church and State, who charged that as a church-related school it should not receive state funds, the following concessions were made.

The school removed all religious symbols from atop its chapel and agreed to strict quotas limiting the number of Methodists serving on its board. Also, it agreed "neither to sponsor nor conduct any religious services," to "remain totally neutral to the spiritual development in a religious sense of its students" and to include no prayers, religious hymns, or sermons in its graduation exercises. Thus another school founded, fostered, and nurtured by faithful Methodists joined that long list of such institutions, many of which were once Baptist, in leaving the original purpose to become just another secular center of learning.

The end is not yet. For in the fall of 1976 at a meeting of the Inter-Agency Council of Texas Baptists, a report was made about attempted federal regulation, even in Baptist schools which had received no federal funds. Abner McCall, president of Baylor University, in a telephone interview said, "The government has made it very clear that whether we get federal aid or not, we're going to get federal control."

In the Inter-Agency Council it was reported "that regulatory agencies of the federal government are making their operations difficult by: financial domination through government rate regulation; requests for photocopies of all records for periods of time based on alleged discrimination; bureaucratic interpretation of laws; demands for immediate compliance to voluminous complex regulations."

At this meeting one of the leaders of the Texas Christian Life Commission said that power tends to beget power. And, said he, the power in the United States is not in the Congress but in the regulatory institutions of the nation.[4]

Southern Baptist theological seminaries, like many others, have never received federal funds. Yet a federal agency ruled that they must abide by the fair employment act in including in its staff and faculty a certain percentage of people without regard to their religion and/or other consideration. This strikes at the very heart of the seminaries' purpose of being. Southwestern Baptist Theological Seminary, Fort Worth, Texas, has volunteered to challenge this ruling in a court test case. At this writing the outcome is not settled. But it vitally affects every seminary regardless of its denominational affiliation.

Another storm cloud of danger on the horizon is in the area of taxation.[5] A report was published of a ruling of the Texas Supreme Court that denies tax exemption to an Episcopal encampment. The court ruled that constitutional tax exemption for an "actual place of worship" does not include the entire 155 acres of an Episcopal church camp in Hood County. The ruling upheld a lower court decision that the Episcopal Diocese of North Texas can receive tax exemption for the camp's open-air chapel and the minister's residence with one acre surrounding each.

This ruling eventually could affect many state Baptist and Southern Baptist encampments, along with those of other denominations. These encampments are used exclusively for religious purposes as defined by the sponsoring bodies. They are the most effective means for leading young people to answer God's call to the ministry as missionaries, pastors, and other related church vocations. Many lay people testify to decisions to dedicate wholly their lives to the Lord in their own chosen vocations. In such an atmosphere the Holy Spirit is better able to do his work in their lives. The cold eyes of government simply cannot make such a spiritual judgment!

Why this sudden change with regard to tax exemption for church property? We cannot overlook the grim phenomenon of a tax-hungry government. Despite campaign oratory to the contrary, the history of taxation generally is not a reduction but an increase, as well as expanse into possibly new areas of revenue. Neither can we ignore the fact of a bureaucratic type of government, with the bureaucrats not being responsible to the electorate. Add to this the fact that they usurp the role of Congress in handing down mandates with the power of law, but these mandates may not be supported by legislation or by the Constitution.

However, in the cases cited we cannot ignore the role of those who have become the victims themselves. For years certain religious groups have held vast properties, including commercial enterprises, with no religious purpose and which were not placed on the tax rolls because they were owned by religious groups. Where property is not used in whole or in part for religious purposes, it should be on the tax rolls—the latter to the degree that it serves no religious purpose. This plus some religious institutions accepting federal funds opened the door for governmental interference. And the innocent suffer with the guilty. The camel got its nose in the tent through lack of foresight and absolute loyalty to the separation principle. Of course, the camel was only too happy to enter bodily. Its strength is such that it could destroy the tent itself.

The storm clouds of governmental interference in religion loom dark on the horizon. It could be that a storm of struggle and sacrifice for this precious principle lies ahead. Will we be as willing to bear the burden as were our forefathers? In the answer to this question may be at stake the ideal of a free church in a free state.

Need for Vigilance

In 1790 John Philpot Curran in a speech on "The Right of Election" said, "It is the common fate of the indolent to see their rights become prey to the active. The condition upon which God hath given liberty to man is eternal vigilance; which condition if he break, servitude is at once the consequence of his crime and the punishment of his guilt." He spoke to his age and to every succeeding one. "Eternal vigilance is the price of freedom" should be the watchword of everyone who cherishes the ideal of a free church in a free state.

Only those who have never known religious liberty or who, having known it, have lost it, fully appreciate it. It is the mother of all freedoms. If it is lost, freedom in other areas of life will soon be lost also. Therefore, the greatest service in this regard that one can render as a Christian and/or a citizen is to be alert to and actively opposed to any governmental encroachment in the field of religious freedom. We must be willing to suffer, if need be, for the preservation of this priceless boon.

In an editorial in the Mississippi *Baptist Record* dated June 16, 1977, Editor Don McGregor wrote, "We may need another Roger Williams [he could have added John Leland, John Waller, Louis Craig, James Childs, and Patrick Henry] in our day. The principle of separation of church and state is being hewn down by broad strokes of the ax. The complex and confusing system of management by bureaucracy that we have instigated in our nation is proving to be a threat to the separation principle. Federal agencies are poking around in a number of areas with regulations that are confusing and implied threats that come with the regulations." He admitted that in some instances "we have brought this problem upon ourselves."

Therefore, it is necessary that every religious institution put its own house in order. Otherwise, it hampers its entire denomination from speaking with a clean conscience and a certain voice. Having done so, religious groups and individuals must speak as with one voice in opposition to any effort of any government agency to fasten its tentacles upon religious bodies and individual consciences. Reversing the words of the traditional wedding vow, we must speak loud and clear:

WHAT GOD HAS PUT ASUNDER LET NO MAN JOIN TOGETHER!

Notes

[1] Baker, p. 24.

[2] Ibid.

[3] Frank Stagg, *The Broadman Bible Commentary* 11 (Nashville: Broadman Press, 1971), p. 210.

[4] Mississippi *Baptist Record,* 9 December 1976.

[5] Texas *Baptist Standard,* 4 October 1976.

9 / The Social Axiom

Love Your Neighbor As Yourself

The word *social* implies the relationships between persons. No one lives in a vacuum. And no man is an island set apart from other people.

Man's Dual Nature

However you may regard man, two things are evident about him. For one thing, he is an individual of infinite worth. The old Greek and Roman civilizations as well as those farther east never recognized this truth. Christ taught it and made it current. Since he lived it has been slowly becoming a part of the spiritual wealth of mankind. And in the present complex social system its message becomes ever more demanding. Man is also a social being with tremendous responsibility. Monasticism in a way stressed the worth of the individual, but it did not value properly the social side of man's nature. The saving of one's own soul and the cultivation of personal Christian virtues are basic facets of the gospel. But beyond that lies the Christian's responsibility for the spiritual and social welfare of others. The ancient Pharisees worked hard at the former, but they gave scant notice to the latter.

In a sense these factors are both contradictory and supplementary. At his creation God made man a distinct individual created in his own image. And yet God said that it is not good for man to be alone (Gen. 1:27; 2:18). So he made "an help meet for him" or one corresponding to him. Though man was made in God's image, a free spiritual person, he was not really complete in his relationships without another free spiritual person at the human level to complement him. Thus it was that from the beginning of the human race, as an individual man was responsible to God for himself; and as a social being he was responsible to God for his fellow beings. Thus God holds us responsible in both relationships.

God's first question to Adam was, "Where art thou?" (Gen. 3:9)
—man's relation to God. His first question to Cain was, "Where is Abel
thy brother?" (Gen. 4:9)—his relation to other people. In both events
man was responsible to God in the situation.

Every individual person is a problem within himself. Add one other
person to the picture and the problems multiply. When a third and a
fourth person are added the problems defy calculation. Adam found this
to be true in his and Eve's relationship with God (Gen. 3:12). With the
addition of Cain and Abel the problems really got out of hand, producing the first murder or fratricide (Gen. 4). These multiple problems are
reflected in God's questions to Adam and Cain. Thus early in the history
of the race man learned of the problems in both his divine and human
relationships.

The Ten Commandments echo this same dual truth (Ex. 20:3–17). As
noted previously, the first four Commandments deal with man's relationship to God; the last six treat his relationship to other people. And in
regard to all ten of the Commandments man is responsible to God for his
actions and attitudes.

In reply to a question as to the great commandment in the law, Jesus
replied, "Thou shalt love the Lord thy God with all thy heart, and with
all thy soul, and with all thy mind. And the second is like unto it, Thou
shalt love thy neighbour as thyself" (Matt. 22:37,39; cf. Deut. 6:5;
Lev. 19:18). Jesus followed the Jewish pattern that these two commandments included the sense of the Decalogue. Indeed, he said that
the meaning of the entire Hebrew Scriptures was contained in them
(Matt. 22:40).

In Luke's account of this conversation (cf. 10:25–37) the questioner
sought to evade the issue of loving one's neighbor by asking Jesus to
identify him. Jews did not regard either Gentiles or Samaritans as
neighbors. In the parable of the good Samaritan Jesus showed that
anyone is my neighbor who needs my help. However, his lesson drawn
from the parable was not to *identify the neighbor,* but to evoke from the
man *how to be a neighbor.* When Jesus asked which of the three people
in the parable "was neighbour unto him that fell among the thieves?"
the lawyer, or expert in interpreting the Mosaic code, replied, "He that

shewed mercy upon him'' (Luke 10:36–37). Note that he did not use the word *Samaritan*. In his Jewish prejudice he would have choked on that word. Jesus told him to ''go, and do thou likewise.''

Someone has noted three social attitudes in this parable. The robbers said, ''What is yours is mine, and I will take it.'' The priest and Levite said, ''What is mine is mine, and I will keep it.'' The Samaritan said, ''What is mine is yours, and I will share it.'' The last is the Christian attitude. As with the early disciples in Jerusalem (Acts 4:33–37), so here, this is not Communism. It is Christian love in action. In neither case was this a forced sharing. Each had control of his own property and could determine how to use it (cf. Acts 5:4). The fact is that Communism has taken a beautiful Christian virtue and warped it into a purely materialistic and political system. That is all the more reason why Christians should demonstrate how sharing works in a purely Christian context.

This brief survey emphasizes the fact that we are individuals of worth and that we are social beings by nature. This survey also shows the proper order in our relationships: We must first be right with God before we can be right with other people. At the same time our attitude toward other people reveals our relationship to God

Importance of the Social Axiom

It is fitting that this axiom should follow the other five—indeed, form a climax for them. Their major thrust is with regard to man's unfettered relationship to God, and this is as it should be. But the sixth axiom binds the whole into a neat package, as it reminds us of the purpose of God that those in a proper relation to him should bear a proper relationship to all others of his people.

The starting point in our religious pilgrimage is to be made right with God. So in a very real sense it begins at Calvary and the empty tomb, where we see what God in Christ has done for us. But that pilgrimage leads us, not into a monastery, but into all the world and unto the end of the age.

''God commendeth his love toward us, in that, while we were yet sinners, Christ died for us'' (Rom. 5:8). The verb rendered ''commendeth" in this context means to show. The present tense means to do it constantly. "Love" (*agape*) is the word for the highest kind of love as seen in God's nature (1 John 4:8). It carries the idea of selflessness. So in the death of his Son the Father showed this attitude toward even those in rebellion against him.

As we study this word (*agape*) in the New Testament we perceive God's love coming down to us; our love in faith returning to God; and, in this relationship, God's love through us reaching out to the whole world. If you follow these movements, you make the sign of the cross. Thus the cross in our lives is individual in that we believe in Christ for ourselves. But it also has an otherness meaning as we are charged to share the gospel with the entire human race. This involves both missions and/or evangelism and ministering to the total needs of men.

The social axiom has always been applicable to men's relationship to each other. But in the modern urbanized society it is especially needed. The first city was built by Cain, who murdered his brother (Gen. 4:17). There is something symbolic in this. For when people are crowded together in a large city they are at the same time drawn apart from one another. "Am I my brother's keeper?" becomes the prevailing attitude. People tend to lose their identity as they become wandering statistics in concrete jungles. This sad situation is compounded by the breeding of crime as many become preying beasts seeking whom they may devour. In such a situation people need to know that they are not forgotten, that someone cares. Neighbors are all about us who have fallen into the hands of the thieves of a social order in which persons lose their identity in the mad rush to exist along the Jericho roads of life. It is under such conditions that Christians need to extend helping hands.

Gaines S. Dobbins spent his life teaching seminary students. His major thrust was to lead them to a practical application of theological truth in a ministry to persons. Thus he declared a conviction born of both academic and practical experience.

> Those of us who live relatively untroubled, undisturbed, peaceful lives may find it difficult to realize how many there are whose lives are troubled, disturbed, and hopelessly unhappy. They may be well-to-do neighbors who put on a bold front. They may be couples who 'have

everything' but peace and happiness. They may be the deprived, the unfortunate, the 'dead-enders' who see nothing ahead but failure. They may be young rebels determined to 'do their own thing' and who are making a tragic mess of it. They may be chanceless children, disowned and unloved, for whom life holds no promise. They may be of a minority race and culture, written off by their advantaged superiors. The list of the troubled grows long; and they are everywhere, near and far.[1]

Yes, it may be difficult for us to realize and to recognize these conditions. But we must do so. And we must reach out to them in the name and spirit of Christ—that is, if we are to be effective evangels and faithful to him who is at the heart of the gospel. He never turned a deaf ear to the calls of those in need. And neither can we, if we would follow in the "footsteps of Jesus."

Nature of the Gospel

What is the gospel anyway? It is a common word in the Christian vocabulary. But what does it entail? Good news? Yes, but good news about what? About God's purpose and plan to change men. But how? As one views the present religious scene, it is evident that there are two prevailing answers to this question.

Around the turn of the century many leading authorities in the field of religious thought faced the future with a rosy optimism. The industrial revolution and the accomplishments of science caused them to feel that the human race stood on the threshold of the golden age. It was thought that by his own bootstraps man had practically picked himself up out of the mire of sin. He stood tall above the jungle law of tooth and talon. As late as 1912 many of the greatest minds were saying that man had so progressed as to make war impossible!

Prior to this time the central note of the gospel had been the salvation of the individual, little more than an escape from the fires of hell. But in this new age many demanded a sociological gospel. They insisted that individualism was a false teaching and that the gospel aims primarily at social results. In many quarters it took the form of an assertion that a change in environment is all that is necessary to effect a change in character. They insisted that the happy are the good. The way to make men good is to make them happy. The way to make them happy is to make them comfortable; good houses to live in, good food to eat, and good clothes to wear are the sum total of the things required to regenerate society. The champions of this *gospel* railed against the churches for failure to insist upon this view.

It was in such an atmosphere that the purely *social gospel* was born. Whatever position one may have held toward it, it helped to awaken the churches to a social concern which for the most part had been lacking. But the battle raged between the advocates of a *social gospel* and a *spiritual gospel*. World War I stunned but did not stop the apostles of the new age. However, the Great Depression of the 1930s, followed by World War II, subsequent wars, and social violence within the nation largely negated the social gospel. In the meantime old-line denominations, including some Baptists, during the storm had broken from their historical moorings and have not yet been anchored to them again. During this storm Southern Baptists continued to adhere to the spiritual gospel; but through the intervening years they have seen certain changes in their view of the nature of the gospel.

In any dispute there are usually three sides: yours, mine, and the right one. That man needs changing is quite evident. Experience of this century demonstrates to us that he must be changed from the inside out, not from the outside in. Simply to transfer a person from one social environment to a better one means only that a sinner has changed his address and social status. There is something radically wrong inside man himself. But once he is changed on the inside, he should become concerned about others. This involves both their inner nature and their outer circumstances. Thus the gospel in its true nature is spiritual, but it also involves social concern. It is a spiritual gospel with social implications. A merely sociological Christianity fails because it ignores the basic law of the Christian faith. To regenerate the individual is the sole condition of permanent moral progress in the social sphere.

However, individual regeneration is not the ultimate goal of evangelism. It is the first necessary step in the direction of producing a Christlikeness in the individual Christian. This calls not only for personal holiness but for involvement in the whole of life in the name of Christ. Its method is to change society through changed people. This involves the initial phase of leading others to Christ. But beyond that, it means to develop and involve them in endeavoring to implant the Christian ethic in the whole of life. Only redeemed people can truly bring Christ's redemptive work to be felt in a social order which, within itself, gives little or no recognition to God.

Thus the *right side* is neither a purely social gospel nor a purely spiritual gospel. It is a combination of the two ideals; but to be successful it must begin with an inner spiritual change of the individual which expresses itself in social concern in all areas of life. Christianity cannot abandon its doctrine of *regenerated individualism* without committing suicide. It is by means of regenerated individuals associated together as churches that Christianity becomes a leaven to transform the social order. This is primary and fundamental.

At the same time churches cannot isolate themselves as little societies of the redeemed, existing in a jungle of forces hostile to every Christian virtue. Regeneration contains in itself the seeds of all righteousness. No moral interest, therefore, lies outside the sphere of the church of Christ. Doubtless much of the failure of the church to leaven the social relations of men has grown out of a lack of recognition of this truth. Furthermore, much of the invasion of the church family by the pagan morés of its social environment may be attributed to the same failure. If the army of the Lord is not on the attack against social evil, the soldiers of Christ may mistake this seeming neutrality as either approval or compromise and thus be led to lie down in the camp of the enemy.

No church is likely to run over its pastor in its onrush to attack the enemy. In most instances it will follow his leadership in a campaign against social evil. The role of the pastor, therefore, carries an ominous responsibility. From him through his pulpit ministry the church must learn that the new birth involves the regeneration of the entire life. Salvation is not a fragment such as being in the ark of safety. It is a call to steer that ark to places of need where church members can rescue the perishing and care for the dying. It is to throw out the lifeline to those who are being engulfed, seemingly for the last time, by the rolling waves of evil not only conceptual but also circumstantial.

Under the pastor's guidance the church should exert a powerful influence upon the state. It cannot and should not usurp the role of the state. But it does take the citizens of the state into itself. It cannot undertake commercial enterprises with wisdom and safety, but it does have the moral and spiritual guidance of businessmen. One of the most serious difficulties to be overcome is the artificial grouping of men with moral ideals to correspond. Politicians have become a professional class with us. Businessmen in like manner in important respects think and act on certain accepted lines and ideals. In both cases the accepted norm is that they operate by rules of their own making, which too often are contrary to Christian ideals. This has no reference to corruption and immorality, even though they are some of the bitter fruit of divorcing their rules from Christian virtue.

For instance, a holder of public office advised his pastor to steer away from politics. "For," said he, "we operate by a different set of rules from yours." Such should not be the case. Now the pastor need not run for public office. But from the throne of his pulpit he should declare God's message that the rules of the Ten Commandments and the ethical principles of Christianity should apply in the halls of state and the marts of trade even as they do within the walls of the church building.

I know of no greater need today than preaching from the Old Testament prophets. So often when we hear the word *prophet* we think of foretelling the future. The Old Testament prophets did do that, but within the context of their preaching to their own generations. *Prophecy* means both foretelling and telling forth. And the latter was the principal role of Bible prophets. They thundered God's judgment upon corrupt politicians and corrupt business people, their oppression of the poor, drunkenness and immorality, and the running sores of an evil social order that paid lip service to God while bowing before idols of materialism.

They did not run for public office or carry on economic pursuits. But they proclaimed God's message to kings and princes, to merchant moguls, and against injustice of the courts toward the helpless poor. They led no organized crusades and manned no picket lines. But instead of humanistic social theories, they spoke with a "thus saith the Lord." Their message of condemnation was always tempered with God's offer of mercy to the repentant. And they called for a turning to the ways of Jehovah. Typical of the golden age of prophecy (eighth century B.C.) was the fearless preaching against social evil by Amos. "But let judgment [justice] run down as waters, and righteousness as a mighty stream" (5:24). And Micah said: "He hath shewed thee, O man, what is good; and what doth the Lord require of thee, but to do justly, and to love mercy, and to walk humbly with thy God?" (6:8). This should not be mistaken for a means of salvation, but as a call to a godly life.

Jesus and the Gospel

This social axiom is affirmed by Jesus' own approach to the gospel. It was to Nicodemus, one of the socially elite, that he said, "Ye must be born again" (John 3:7). This involves a radical change from inside out. Outward reformation is only a veneer. At the other end of the Jewish social scale Jesus did not attack Zacchaeus for his dishonesty. He led him to faith in him, and Zacchaeus rectified his wrongs (Luke 19:1–10). Had Jesus attacked Zacchaeus and his evil system of extortion in the name of tax collection, he would have gained the praise rather than the censure of the people. But he would have lost Zacchaeus. Rather, he won him to himself. And in place of a crooked chief publican, he presented the people with a Christian tax commissioner. He adapted his method to the need.

The case of Nicodemus belies the claim that education, wealth, and affluence can produce new people with new values and goals in life. This Jewish teacher had all of these; yet he was a seeker after a deeper experience. At the same time the case of Zacchaeus demonstrates that one cannot sink so low in life but that God loves and cares. The one says that no person should presume; the other that no one should despair.

In the case of the woman of Samaria Jesus went beyond the closed circle of Jewry to deal with an outsider who was in dire need (John 4). It would be difficult to imagine a situation fraught with greater difficulties. This instance literally bristles with prejudice: race, religion, sex, moral separation, and scorn. Yet patiently Jesus overcame all of these as he led this woman from her scorn for Jews (v. 9) and local pride (v. 12) to respect for Jesus (vv. 15–19), through her diversion to faith in him (vv. 20–26) which changed her into a bearer of the good news about him (vv. 28–29). Her timid witness resulted also in many of her towns-people believing in Jesus as their Savior (vv. 39–42). Doubtless the seed sown here later yielded a rich harvest in the revival which resulted from Philip's preaching in Samaria (Acts 8).

It is evident from these examples that in his ministry Jesus was not limited by manmade distinctions. Where need existed there was the Great Physician seeking to meet that need (Mark 2:15–17). He ate with both publicans and sinners and with Pharisees not because he agreed with their life-styles but because they needed his ministry (Luke 11:37; 15:1–2). He met the needs of noblemen (John 4:46–53), lepers (Luke 17:11–19), the lame (Luke 6:6–10; John 5:1–9), and the blind (Luke 18:35–43; John 9:1–7). He cast out demons from Jews and Gentiles (Matt. 12:22; Mark 5:1–15). On the same day he healed the son of a Roman centurion and the Jewish mother-in-law of Peter (Matt. 8:5–15).

No one can be true to the picture of Jesus and say that he was indifferent to human need other than the spiritual. He came to save the whole man: his soul, so he died for him; his mind, so he taught him; his body, so he healed him. But he did recognize that the proper starting place is the saving of the individual soul. He forgave the paralytic's sins before healing his body (Mark 2:1–12). He called people to himself, trained them, and then sent them forth to minister (Mark 6:7–13,30; Luke 10:1–11). Peter was like so many Christians and churches. He wanted to stay in the mountain with the Lord. But Jesus reminded him in his actions that there was human need to be met in the valley (Matt. 17:4,14–21).

The nature of salvation as involving regeneration, sanctification, and glorification calls for more than regenerated individualism. For sanctification involves one's serving of others in both evangelism and social ministry. And as we shall see later in this chapter, the eschatological nature of glorification is related to the temporal experiences in regeneration and sanctification.

Role of the Church

It is impossible to separate the role of the Christian from that of the church. Through the individual members of a given fellowship the church's impact will be felt. At the same time this concept, while involving the work of one church, also calls for the voluntary coopera- tive endeavor of many churches. To borrow a phrase from the title of Foy Valentine's book, Christians should *Believe and Behave*.

One of the greatest developments among Southern Baptists during the past generation has been the emergence of a growing sense of social responsibility. While maintaining a strong emphasis upon the need for individual regeneration, the churches and denominational groupings have more and more accepted Christian responsibility in the social order. The latter has not resulted in a lessening of evangelistic zeal. But it is recognized as a part of the overall Christian task. That Southern Baptists have long had this social consciousness to a large degree is seen in the sponsorship of educational institutions, orphanages, and hospitals at various levels within the denomination. The purpose of these institu- tions is to render social service with the "Christian plus." Schools and hospitals are two of the most effective foreign mission efforts. They provide needed services as such, but they also give an entrée to the gospel that otherwise might not be available. In the spirit of Jesus these services have the ultimate goal of reaching people for him.

The Christian Life Commission may well be called the *social con- science* of the Southern Baptist Convention. Though at times it has been through rough waters, this agency, along with its corresponding bodies in some state conventions, has helped to lead the denomination to support both legal and social efforts in the problem-ridden period of the 1940–1977 era. Perhaps one of the high-water marks, though controver- sial at the time, was this Commission's leadership which resulted in the Southern Baptist Convention calling upon Baptists to cooperate in the landmark decision of the United States Supreme Court concerning school desegregation.

It should be noted, however, that in social strife the role of the church

has been misunderstood. Social and political activists have accused
churches and denominations of being indifferent to social injustice; the
reason being that their pastors and other members did not join picket
lines or other such demonstrations. As noted previously, Jesus did not
picket the home of Zacchaeus. Neither did he join one brother against
the other in a dispute over their father's estate. Instead he preached to
both about the sin of covetousness (Luke 12:13–21). A church can do no
better than to follow the example of its Lord.

In its prophetic role the church should cry out against every form of
injustice, corruption, and man's inhumanity to man. Whatever prosti-
tutes and violates the well-being of people made in God's image is
legitimate game for the volleys of God's prophets. The enemies of Jesus
called him "a friend of publicans and sinners" (Luke 7:34). The
criticism was really a compliment. It is no wonder that such people
came to hear him (Luke 15:1)! In the three great parables in Luke 15
Jesus exposed the hands-off policy of the Pharisees and scribes and
showed that social outcasts were the objects of God's love.

However, churches cannot be content merely with pronouncements.
They should develop their people and send them forth into society to be
salt and light to a decaying, bedarkened social order. For salt to heal
and/or prevent decay it must come into contact with its object. But in
doing so it never ceases to be salt. Likewise, Christians must be in the
world as instruments of Christ, but must never become a part of its evil
system. They must be willing to get their hands dirty, as it were, as they
minister in the Savior's name.

Furthermore, the churches must foster positive efforts to minister to
the needs of the unfortunate. They must minister personally to the
up-and-outs as well as the down-and-outs, each in the area of his needs.
We should never forget that the same Lord who ministered to the needs
of the woman at the well also ministered to Nicodemus. To neglect
either is to fall short of our responsibility. A person may be held down
by the chains of greed as well as by the chains of poverty. Someone said
that "if a man is imperfect who is apart from the divine, so is a man
imperfect who is apart from the human."

The true imitation of Christ consists not in asking "What would Jesus do?'' merely, but in asking ''What would Jesus have us to do?'' Christ cannot be copied. He is less a model for us than an archetype. We may imitate but not copy him. To copy Christ would be to attempt to cure the blind by anointing his eyes with clay mixed with his own spittle. To imitate him is to devise measures legal and otherwise to relieve and try to prevent blindness. To copy Christ is to attempt to feed the hungry thousands by a miraculous multiplication of loaves and fishes. To imitate Christ is to labor for equitable social conditions, just laws, and equal privileges for men and women as they earn their daily bread. To imitate Christ is not to take sides with labor against capital or with capital against labor, but rather to teach capital and labor to perform their respective duties.

Christ did not deal directly with human rights, though no teacher ever did so much to establish them. He dealt with human duties, knowing that this was the point needing emphasis. He began by setting people right with God, then proceeded to get them right between themselves. He ever sought to lead people to love God absolutely and their neighbors as themselves. He knew that human life was safe only as human attitudes were right, that society will be pure only as social beings are pure, that property is not endangered only as people guard themselves from covetousness, and that families are secure only as they are secured in mutual love and loyalty to Christ and to one another.

But at the same time we are disloyal to Christ as long as we regard the social, political, and commercial world as a foreign country to the Christian. To regard this world as utterly cursed of God is virtually to deliver it over to Satan's dominion. This is nothing more than monasticism. Even if worst comes to worst, if civilization itself should fall, Christians should be found ''where cross the crowded ways of life,'' enabling people to hear the voice of the Son of man and to see him at work meeting their total needs.

Christ cannot be claimed as the special patron of any particular reform movement. But sin on both sides is his concern. Little systems have their day and then cease to be. They grow to maturity and flourish like the trees in the forest and then, dying, fall piecemeal to fertilize the soil below. Only the Lord's church endures through the ages. And he ever wills that it shall be *in* the world but not *of* it, declaring and demonstrating his truth and leading men to follow it. In the meantime, God is the sun which warms the soil in which lie slumbering the seeds of his kingdom, and he causes them to germinate and grow up to supply spiritual bread for mankind.

Principle of Final Judgment

In his picture of the final judgment in Matthew 25:31–46 Jesus set forth the principle of that judgment. The key factor is the manner in which people have or have not ministered to other people in need. This should not be construed to mean that we are saved or lost by what we do or do not do in social service. Rather, it means that people reveal their attitude and relationship to Jesus by their attitude and relationship to needy people about them.

This thought is found elsewhere in the New Testament. James challenged us to demonstrate our faith in Christ by our works (2:8). While it is not the whole of religion, he said, "Pure religion and undefiled before God and the Father is this, To visit the fatherless and widows in their affliction, and to keep himself unspotted from the world" (1:27). He probed our hearts as he asked, "What doth it profit, my brethren, though a man say he hath faith, and have not works? can faith [that kind of faith] save him? If a brother or sister be naked, and destitute of daily food, and one of you say unto them, Depart in peace, be ye warmed and filled; notwithstanding ye give them not those things which are needful to the body; what doth it profit?" (2:14–16).

It is no wonder that this little epistle is called a practical application of Christianity. Some would see a conflict between Paul and James on faith. Not so. They simply look at the same thing with different emphases. And in what may well be Paul's greatest single statement about salvation by grace through faith (Eph. 2:8–10), he said that we are not saved by or out of (*ek*) ourselves or our good works as the source. But note that we are saved "unto [as the goal] good works, which God hath before ordained that we should walk [order our manner of life] in [*en*] them" or in the sphere of them. In 1 Corinthians 6:20 Paul exhorted Christians to "glorify God in your body" (the remainder of v. 20 is not in the best manuscripts). We are to glorify God in our bodies by ministering to the bodies and other needs of men.

Referring back to James' words, we are reminded of the old story of a devout man and his son. One day the father saw him coming out of the smokehouse with a ham under one arm and a side of bacon under the other. When he asked his son what he was doing, the son replied, "I'm taking these to the Widow Jones. I'm helping God answer *your* prayers that he will feed her and her orphaned children." Indeed, can we really pray about a matter when, having the means to satisfy it, we do not do so? In such a case we should pray for God to burden our hearts about it to the point that we will meet the needs ourselves, using the means that God has placed at our disposal. And we should do it in his name.

Where human need exists and we have the means by which to meet it, a slap on the back of a needy person and a hearty "God bless you" are nothing short of hypocrisy. In such a situation one's *prayers* hardly reach the ceiling. Rather than to pray pious prayers, God expects his people to do something about it. He never does through a miracle what he can do through a man!

First John 4:20–21 reads, "If a man say, I love God, and hateth his brother, he is a liar: for he that loveth not his brother whom he hath seen, how can he love God whom he hath not seen? And this commandment have we from him, That he who loveth God love his brother also."

This brings us back to Jesus' words about the judgment in Matthew 25. In this account the "sheep" are invited to inherit the kingdom. But why or on what basis? The sheep inherited the kingdom because they had done things for Jesus. In reply to their question of surprise as to when they had done this, Jesus said, "Inasmuch as ye have done it unto one of the least of these my brethren, ye have done it unto me" (v. 40). On the other hand, the goats were sent into everlasting fire because they had not done these things to other people—and so, not to Jesus (vv. 41–45).

Two things are evident in this picture. For one thing, Jesus identifies himself with the needy. The only way we can minister to him bodily is through ministering to them. Again, one's attitude toward those who need his service expresses his attitude toward Jesus. Had Jesus been present in person, these would have treated him the same way—either ministered to him or ignored him. We demonstrate our characters with respect to Christ as we do the same with respect to needy people. For emphasis it should be repeated. We are not saved through social service, but through it or the lack of it we reveal whether or not we are saved.

Yes, the social axiom says that we should love our neighbors as ourselves. The demanding question is not "Who is my neighbour?" It is "How may I be a neighbor?"

Note

[1] Gaines S. Dobbins, *Good News to Change Lives* (Nashville: Broadman Press, 1976), p. 115.

10 / Facing the Future

We must always speak of the future with a big IF: *If* the Lord delays his return. But he specifically told his people to be busy about his work until he comes.

The Lord's Return

Innately man wants to know what lies in the future. With Christians this desire centers largely upon the time of the Lord's return. Through the centuries efforts have been made to determine the time of it, but to no avail. Perhaps there is more study to that effect today than ever before.

It is of interest, therefore, that the New Testament does *not* set a date. Its emphasis is upon constant expectancy. "Watch therefore: for ye know not what hour your Lord doth come" (Matt. 24:42). "Watch" is a command to be constantly on guard, alertly looking for his return. Paul and other New Testament writers wrote in terms of their own generation. They were not mistaken but were doing exactly what Jesus commanded. Some generation will be living when it happens. Theirs was the only living generation at the time. Every generation, even ours, should follow their example.

In Mark 13:32 Jesus said that even he did not know the time of his return. He spoke only what the Father told him. He had not spoken to him about this. Jesus never spoke of his return in terms of time but of condition. "When" refers primarily to condition. When the condition is right, that is the time (Matt. 24:28,32). The most definite statement of Jesus as to the time of his return refers to condition. "And this gospel of the kingdom shall be preached in all the world for a witness unto all nations; and then shall the end come" (Matt. 24:14). We are to be busy

161

producing this condition. The time we can leave with God.

It is by definite design that God does not reveal the end of time to us. If we knew that it would not occur for a century or a thousand years, what incentive would that be for godly living and faithful service? But since it may happen before I draw the next breath, that should serve as both a warning and an encouragement: a warning not to do anything we would not want to be found doing when he comes; an encouragement to be found busy about his work when he comes.

We hear much today about the Lord's return being near. *It is always near!* But certain signs often cited to this effect (wars, rumors of wars, famines, pestilences, and earthquakes) are not signs. Jesus was specifically warning us not to be misled by false signs (Matt. 24:4–7). These are but a part of history. The one sign he gave comes in verse 14.

It should be noted that in Matthew 24—25 and parallel passages in Mark and Luke Jesus was answering three questions: "When shall these things be [destruction of Jerusalem]? and what shall be the sign of thy coming, and of the end of the world?" (24:3). Careful exegesis is necessary to understand which question he is treating at a given point; at times they may even overlap.

One thing is certain. Jesus' return is nearer today than it was yesterday. Another is that we do possess for the first time in history the means for preaching the gospel to the whole world *in a day*. And for each of us another fact looms large. Even should the Lord's return at the end of the age be far distant, insofar as we are concerned he will come for each of us at our death in a relatively short time. So, leaving the end time with the Lord, we should be busy about his work.

Acts 1:7–8 sums up the matter. Jesus was on his way to Olivet for his ascension. The disciples asked if at that time he would "restore again the kingdom to Israel" (v. 6). He replied, "It is not for you to know the times and seasons [fine points and periods or details as to the time of his return], which the Father hath put in his own power. But ye shall receive power, after that the Holy Ghost [Spirit] is come upon you: and ye shall be witnesses unto me both in Jerusalem, and in all Judaea, and in Samaria, and unto the uttermost part of the earth." In essence he said that we are to leave with the Father that which only he can do; and we are to be busy about the task which by his grace and wisdom only we can do. It is in this concept that we speak of facing the future. And our Jerusalem is where we are.

In a very real sense for the Christian's work, there is no time to call the *future*. Even as we speak of it, by the time we say it, it is the *present*. Thus so far as the Lord's work is concerned, the future is now! It is the abiding present. The important thing is not what we plan to do in some far-distant, future time. But what are we doing for the Lord *now*? Of course, we must envision the unfolding years and plan for them as to what we will be doing a day, a year, or a decade from now should the Lord delay his return. However, the world cannot wait. Some years ago the executive secretary of the Foreign Mission Board said, ''If we have a message for the world, we must declare it now. For doors for the gospel are being closed by non-Christian powers all over the world.''

Applying the Axioms

In this light it should be recognized that the foregoing axioms are not merely academic in nature. They are vibrant principles to guide us in living for the Lord. The competency of the soul in religion entails the responsibility of the soul in religion.

Since God is sovereign, he has the right to command his people. The equal right of all men to direct access to God means that we should make known that right to all men and defend it against any interference. Equal privilege in the church makes every believer equally responsible for what his church is doing in carrying out the Great Commission. Free believers are under obligation to obey God when he commands. A free church in a free state forbids churches to expect governments to do their God-given work for them. And we cannot love our neighbor as ourselves if we ignore his physical and spiritual needs.

In speaking of servanthood Jesus said, ''If ye know these things, happy are ye if ye do them'' (John 13:17). He assumed that the disciples *knew*. But would they *do*? Certainly, Christians cannot plead ignorance as to God's will in the matter at hand. We are accountable to him if we fail to do it.

Challenging Problems

In any way that we view the future, it is fraught with problems. We live in a problem-perplexed present. And the future promises no relief from these problems. Instead, they are likely to become more expansive and intensive. And they will become increasingly a challenge to the people of God. It would be folly of the worst kind for us to refuse to acknowledge that they exist or to look in the other direction in hope that they will disappear. No longer can any one part of the world pull in its boundaries and live in isolation. For modern technology has made the world a neighborhood. Thus we may well ask as to the problems we face and, in doing so, determine to be good neighbors to the world.

However, an equally foolish attitude would be to look at the enormity of our task and then simply throw up our hands in helpless despair with the result that we do not try. We would do well to take to heart the words of Jesus in the Sermon on the Mount—literally, "Be not overly anxious [distracted] looking toward tomorrow, for tomorrow will be overly anxious about itself. Sufficient to the day is its own evil" (Matt. 6:34). Many people are driven to distraction by worrying about the future when actually we should live one day at a time. It is like piling on the table before you the total amount of food you will eat in a whole year. Obviously your reaction would be that you could not eat it all at once. So you do not eat a bite. On the other hand, when it is placed before you in equitable portions one meal at a time, you eat it with delight.

In like fashion we must not despair of the foreboding future. We must live it one day at a time, doing our best each day. The final note of verse 34 simply means that we should not borrow tomorrow's trouble today. We have all we can handle today. Let tomorrow's trouble take its turn. And never forget our Lord's promise in John 16:33. "In the world ye shall have tribulation [be in a tight place with seemingly no way out]; but be of good cheer [courage]; I have overcome [fully conquered] the world." In this light let us look at the problems before us.

An independent research organization, Worldwatch Institute, received a grant from the United Nations Fund for Population Activities in an effort to determine the crises apparent today. From their report Bob Hughes, assistant editor of *Perspective* magazine, summarized some of the salient facts. I am indebted to him for the following statistics.

One of the greatest problems is the population explosion out of which most other problems grow. It is no accident that those areas with the greatest population also have the most misery and need. In 1976 the world's population was about four billion. At the present rate of growth, it is doubling every thirty-seven years. The battle to reach the zero mark in population growth at this point seems to be a losing struggle. So world planners must view their work in this light.

And this fact alone is producing compounded problems. One concerns nutrition. If a significant portion of the earth's people are starving now, what will be the picture with eight billion in 2013, sixteen billion in 2050, thirty-two billion in 2087, and more than a trillion in a few centuries? One of the main sources of high-quality protein is fish. From 1950 to 1970 the world's catch of fish more than tripled, from twenty-one million tons to seventy million tons. But since then the catch has declined. The oceans are being fished faster than the fish can reproduce. And as water pollution increases we are told that we can say good-bye to ocean plankton, which is the starting point for all sea life.

Add to this the fact that grain consumption increased per capita from 583 pounds in 1960 to 631 pounds in 1973. With the continued population growth, annual per capita production of grain is now dropping by 35 pounds per year. At the present malnutrition is linked to the spread of disease. Infant malnutrition causes brain damage, making tomorrow's retarded adults.

Health care is nonexistent for half the world's population. Cancer is now the leading cause of death among children under fifteen in the United States. But according to the United States Public Health Service, an incurable disease called *schistosomiasis,* which is carried by parasites in water, is now "the greatest plague in the world." Forty percent of all Egyptians are infected and their lives shortened. Due to the rapid growth in population the fight to provide adequate clean drinking water has been lost. In India less than one-tenth of the villages have clean drinking water.

Ecology is one of the world's greatest problems. And it is more than smog over large cities. One of the most beautiful bodies of water on earth is the Mediterranean Sea. Yet it is the sewer for more than 400 million people. It may become a *dead sea*. In Japan mercury in industrial waste produces a limb-twisting disease.

Someone has said that it is a terrible thing to waste a mind. Yet between 1950 and 1976 illiterates increased from 700 million to 800 million. In Asia, Africa, and South America the building of schools and the finding of teachers are far behind the population growth. Millions of children become adults who can neither read nor write.

In America with its wide expanses of land it is difficult to realize the overcrowding in many parts of the world. Yet in Java people are moving into volcano craters in search for land and living space. The horrible death of 168 people in a tidal wave in Bangladesh was due to these people living in low coastal areas for want of land elsewhere.

In some poor nations overgrazing by livestock causes erosion and the abandonment of land. According to the United Nations, more than a quarter of a million acres of farmland are lost annually to the Sahara desert. This desert waste is creeping northward toward the Mediterranean as people there frantically endeavor to feed families in ever-increasing numbers.

We are familiar with the energy crisis, which warns us that taken-for-granted sources of energy are in dwindling supply. But even the humble energy source called firewood, the primary source of fuel for more than one-third of mankind, is in increasingly short supply. Due to pushing back the forests by an increasing population and the expanding of desert areas, in some parts of the world villagers must make a day's journey in order to get a single bundle of wood.

Look at these figures on deforestation. "Forests that once covered a third of Morocco, Tunisia, and Algeria now cover scarcely a tenth of the area they once did. The Ivory Coast rain forest has been diminished by 30 percent from 1956 to 1966. In Java, as little as 12 percent of the lush island still has tree cover. In the Philippines where the forest once covered nearly half the land, it now covers less than a fifth. With deforestation comes floods, erosion, deserts—and the inability of the land to support human life."

Under such conditions people are crowding into the cities. It is estimated that soon half of the world's urban population will live in slums, where crime breeds and where children grow up without privacy, education, light, and cleanliness. In places like Ghana and Algiers, twenty to thirty people live in a single house. It has been suggested that similar crowding is one major contributing cause for the crime rate in America's large cities being eleven times that of rural areas.

Admittedly this is a grim picture of the world in which we live. But the first step toward meeting its challenge is to recognize the problem. The manager of a large automotive assembly plant was asked about the future in light of the energy crisis. He replied that the automotive industry is already working on it. And, said he, "When the time comes to meet it, we'll be ready."

Will the Lord's people be ready? More to the point, are we willing to meet the challenge? Of course, the gigantic nature of the problems means that the united effort of governments and industry is needed. But as constituted groups Christians cannot, must not, ignore their part in this war for the survival of the human race. We must learn in a hitherto unknown scope how to be neighbors to the world. And we must provide the *Christian plus* to our ministry. Even the preaching of the gospel to such an exploding population will tax to the limit our power and participation. William Lyon Phelps said, "One man finds an obstacle a stumbling block; another finds it a stepping stone." Which is it to us?

Blessings and Responsibilities

In modern history nowhere in all the world has evangelical Christianity grown more rapidly and become stronger than in the United States of America. Enjoying religious liberty, Christians have been free to preach, teach, and make disciples. For instance, one cannot separate this fact from another which shows that there are more Baptists in this nation than in all the rest of the world. And since there is no established church the various denominations have developed a spirit of self-reliance fiscally and otherwise. If the Christians of this nation, therefore, have the will to do so, by the power of the Holy Spirit they can rise to meet the challenge of a needy world. We have the manpower, money power, and the God power that can enable us to play a significant role in meeting the challenge of the future.

We need to learn the lessons of holy history in which God has moved significantly to meet the deepest needs of mankind. Abraham stands as the headwaters of a mighty stream. By way of review recall that in ancient Ur of the Chaldees God called him. "Get thee out of thy country, and from thy kindred, and from thy father's house, unto a land that I will shew thee. And I will make of thee a great nation, and I will bless thee . . . and thou shalt be a blessing" (Gen. 12:1–2). He did not tell him the name of his destination; neither did he furnish him a road map for his journey. His road map was hidden in the mind and heart of God.

The early Christians were given a seemingly impossible task to take the world for Christ. But they were to learn that what is impossible for man is possible with God. Indeed, someone has said that we never test the power of God until we attempt the impossible. So greatly were these early believers blessed and so much were they a blessing that, in less than three centuries after Jesus gave the Great Commission, there were so many Christians in the Roman Empire that the pagan emperor saw the expediency of espousing their cause.

During this period many other religions also vied for the hearts of men. One historian has said that Christianity won the battle because Christians outthought, outworked, outloved, outsuffered, and outdied the devotees of other religions.

Now it is not my thesis that the United States or Christian people in it are a modern Israel such as ancient Israel. First Peter 2:1–10 shows that the true Israel of God is made up of Christians of all lands (cf. Rev. 5:9–10). But one cannot help at least to see a parallel. Our nation has become the crossroads of the world. It has wealth beyond the fondest dreams of ancient emperors. God has spent hundreds of years in preparing us. Could it be that he is looking for our nation, and especially the Christians in it, to meet the present crisis that faces the entire race? It is something to ponder. Our blessings have become our responsibility!

Basic Need Is Spiritual

As we recall the problems facing mankind today, it is not a mere preachment to say that man's basic need is spiritual. This is true because it involves eternal values as over against temporal ones. Furthermore, a people's spiritual base definitely and directly affects their entire attitude toward life. Is it any accident that man's greatest material progress has been made in those parts of the earth where Christianity is predominant? Or, to go one step further, even in those areas the greatest progress has been made where an active evangelical Christianity is found.

Freedom of the spirit, not only in relation to the state but also in relation to God's dealings with people, liberates the whole person. Even where a scientist may not be a Christian, he works in an atmosphere flavored with Christian ideals.

On the other hand, the most nonprogressive areas of the earth are those where even the predominant Christianity stifles freedom of expression or soul competency. Otherwise such areas are dominated by either animism, Islam, or cultural pagan religions. This is not to equate the industrialism of the West with the Christian faith. Americanism as such is not synonymous with Christianity.

When in Korea some years ago missionaries told us that one of their greatest obstacles in leading the people to adopt new and better methods of doing ordinary things was their religion. It involved the worship of their ancestors. To use methods other than theirs would reflect against them.

This same problem exists in India. Having traveled through that nation, having seen the hunger, abject misery, and poverty, we went on to London. At a luncheon Mrs. Hobbs sat next to a man who had recently retired after thirty-five years as a missionary in India. She spoke to him about what we had seen. He said that the only way to solve India's food problem is to teach the people better methods of farming. "If we could teach the farmers to plow a furrow six inches deep rather than three inches deep, they could double their food production. But they will not do it. Their ancestors, because of their primitive plows, made a furrow only three inches deep, and to plow one six inches deep would reflect upon their ancestors." He added that the hope of the future is that the younger generation is beginning to adopt more modern methods of farming.

It is evident, therefore, that basically the problem is a spiritual one. And it is at this point that Christian people can make their greatest contribution. This does not mean that we should immediately put an end to "Care" packages or to direct Christian relief programs. It is a case of these things we ought to do, but not to leave the other undone. You should not turn a hungry man from your door. But having fed him, you can help him more by leading him to Christ and then giving him a job or by teaching him to help himself. We should feed people's bodies, but we should not send them away with hungry souls.

Christians cannot be true to Christ and at the same time shun their responsibility for the world's hurt. The feeding of the five thousand provides a mirror into which we should look. The disciples recognized that the people were hungry. But they told Jesus to send them away that they might themselves buy food. They recognized no responsibility for their plight. But Jesus said, "Give ye them to eat" (Mark 6:37). Then Philip immediately reminded him of the exhorbitant cost (John 6:7). To materially minded people money spent in spiritual ministry is a "waste" (Mark 14:4). Then Jesus told them to use what was available. So with five barley cakes and three small dried fish, food of poor people, plus the power of Jesus, they fed the multitude and had plenty of food left over.

Do you see yourself in this mirror? It is not enough for us to recognize the situation and analyze the problem or to feel that we have discharged our responsibility by sending a needy world away to look out for itself. Neither can we do so by sending them to governmental bodies or by contributing to the Red Cross or some other relief agency. As citizens we should do this. But as *Christians* we should do more. For Jesus still says, "Give ye them to eat." If the Christian people of the United States would give through their churches a minimum of the tithe, to say nothing about offerings, the amount of money available for world service, missionary and otherwise, would be immense. It is not that we lack the means but we lack the will to do. If God's people have the will to do and under the Lord's leadership gear themselves for the work, God will supply the means—through his people.

Available Resources

Earlier in this study it was concluded that the wave of the future seems to be centered in denominationalism. If this is a correct position, it naturally follows that the responsibility for meeting the challenge of the future is incumbent upon denominations and/or conventions. For the most part each one already has at its disposal at least the framework of organization necessary to meet the challenge both in our own nation and in other parts of the world. It is evident that in so gigantic a task these organizations must be increased in strength in both personnel and institutions designed to serve in meeting the challenge. Where there are areas of common interest it may be desirable to coordinate efforts. This would call for joint planning by those charged with leadership in specific areas.

For instance, I have observed that on foreign mission fields the divisions along denominational lines are not so sharply drawn as they are at the home base. That is not to say that any group compromises its doctrinal position. But in lands where Christians are decidedly in the minority, evangelical groups provide spiritual companionship, fellowship, and strength for each other. As small Christian islands in an ocean of paganism, the missionaries realize that the task is larger than all of them combined. And while each group pursues its work in its own way, they are made stronger by the presence of others who have the same ultimate goal of bearing witness for Christ.

As we think about available resources we naturally recognize the presence and power of God. He does not send his people on impossible missions. By our strength alone the task before us is an impossible one. But when we reckon with the power of God the picture changes altogether. For what God says, he can do. And he proposes to do it through his people.

During the early decades of painful growth and persecution we may well imagine the Christians asking questions. Has God been dethroned and Christ defeated? Is the devil on the throne of the universe? Does God know what is happening to us? Does he care? And, even worse, does he know and care but is powerless to act? It was in this historical context that the Lord told John to *look up*! Do not look about you at what is happening on earth! Look up and see what is happening in heaven! When he looked, he saw that God was still on his throne. And he was being continuously praised by the hosts of heaven for his creative work. Then in Revelation 5 John saw the Lamb being praised for his redemptive work.

God is still saying to his people, "Do not look about! Look up!" Despite the problems of earth, God still reigns and in Christ is guiding history toward the accomplishment of his redemptive purpose. We are both the products of and instruments in that purpose.

So the question is not the immensity of the problem; it is whether we will be willing to act in the day of the Lord's power. It is a truism that one man plus God is a majority. In this assurance we should muster our forces for the fray.

With the assurance of the presence and power of God, we are now ready to look at our resources available at the human level. However, we should keep in mind that when placed in the hands of God they are transformed into spiritual resources of infinite worth and ability. As a Southern Baptist I will view them from that standpoint. The principles involved may be applied to any other Christian body. Thus they may be considered as guidelines by which to examine the resources available to any group that endeavors to rise to meet the challenge of world need.

In 1977 Southern Baptists launched a program called Bold Mission Thrust. Its goal is to preach the gospel to every person on this earth by the year 2000. Is this an impossible dream? Before answering too quickly, consider several factors.

For one thing, the need is real. We have noted that the grim picture facing us is basically spiritual in nature. Men primarily need a new nature. The underlying problem of the human race is sin. Because of the sin of Adam, God said, "Cursed is the ground for thy sake" or because of what he had done (Gen. 3:17). From that moment to the present man has had to contend in the natural order to provide for his physical needs.

When man lost his fellowship with God, somehow nature itself became out of harmony with God and his benevolent purpose. In Romans 8 Paul said that the redemption of the natural order waits for the redemption of man. These are things beyond our comprehension. But experience proves that a social order which at least recognizes the true God is better able to cope with the hostility of nature.

Go where you will in the earth and you find one word upon men's lips—freedom. This is related to a more abundant life. Frankly, the rebellion against colonialism in underprivileged areas of the earth is largely the fruit of the gospel. Missionaries have taught these people their dignity before God and the right to freedom and a better life. Unfortunately, we have given the patient just enough of the remedy to make him sick. We have by our example and news media led these people to equate the abundant life with material possessions. They struggle for freedom without knowing its true nature. We need to give the patient the entire dose of the gospel that he may relate himself with the true meaning of Jesus' words about making men free and giving them the abundant life.

Governments and other material agencies may feed and treat men's bodies and provide the material necessities of life; but only those who minister to them in Christian love can enable them to find the real solution to their needs.

Since we are looking at the broader picture of world need, we will present it more from the standpoint of world missions. We have the spiritual and material resources with which to meet the need. We have the manpower and the money power if only they are dedicated to God. What is lacking is a sense of responsibility and mission. If business enterprises can send people over the world in search for raw materials and markets, why should not God's people send armies of men and women bearing the glad tidings of the gospel? No one denomination can do it alone, but if all of them, each in its own way, would lengthen their cords and strengthen their stakes, the need could be met.

Of course, it is assumed that those who go should preach Christ in all his fullness. For no other message will suffice. He and he alone is the Savior. During his first Roman imprisonment Paul noted that people were preaching Christ with varied motives. Yet "Christ is preached; and I therein do rejoice, yea, and will rejoice" (Phil. 1:18). Denominations may differ at many points. But so long as they preach Christ as the one and only complete Savior, to that extent all believers should rejoice.

Many years ago on a Sunday afternoon I turned on the radio, not knowing the nature of the program. A man was preaching a simple gospel sermon on Christ as the Savior of sinful people. Failing to recognize the voice, I thought to myself, "He must be a Baptist preacher." By the time he had finished I was thoroughly convinced of that idea. To my surprise the announcer said, "You have been listening to Monsignor Fulton J. Sheen on 'The Catholic Hour.' " He said not one word about his church's traditions but stayed with the gospel. Though we would have differed about the traditions, we were in agreement about the heart of the gospel. That is the only message that will meet the needs of heart-hungry people.

Last year a small group of Southern Baptists had a luncheon conference with President Carter, a Baptist layman. As a result he was invited to prepare a videotape message on his concern for worldwide witnessing for the 1977 Southern Baptist Convention. In this message he challenged his fellow Baptists that within five years they would have five thousand missionaries on foreign fields, almost double the number at the time. The ultimate goal would be twenty-five thousand. His challenge was issued against the background of the fact that a much smaller group (The Latter-Day Saints of Jesus Christ or the Mormons) have more than 26,000 believers who volunteer to give two years of full-time mission service at their own expense.

Noting that we have only 172 missionary journeymen under a similar volunteer program (but financed by the denomination), he pointed out that more people could be available for temporary journeyman service: seminary professors, pastors and other church personnel, young people, widows, and retired people (pastors and others), many of whom could finance their own expenses. We could also expect people from business, medicine, technological fields, and other professions. President Carter pledged his own support to such an effort.

Albert McClellan, program planning director of the Southern Baptist

Executive Committee, said of this challenge: "I think Mr. Carter represents something that is latent in all of us, and that is a certain kind of enthusiasm which, if it burns brightly enough, will catch the world on fire . . . . Many of our churches have become so preoccupied with the business of building churches at home that they have given little regard to what is happening abroad.

"We cannot survive as the missionary Baptist church in that way—there is just no future apart from the mission task."

It is assumed that the primary thrust in missions both domestic and foreign will be to bring the gospel to bear upon people's hearts—that evangelism, healing, and teaching ministries will not only be continued but must be enlarged. At the same time we should recognize that there is no skill used to earn a legitimate livelihood that cannot also be used to serve the Lord in the sphere of missions. In Nigeria we found an architect serving as a full-time missionary. His responsibility was to draw blueprints and supervise the erection of new buildings, as well as to maintain already-existing ones. Of course, he, like other profession-ally trained missionaries, also preached in churches. In some cases those trained in agriculture and other related fields are found. And why not? Whether they be full-time missionaries or journeymen, they can open the door to the gospel. If we send teachers, doctors, and nurses, why not those trained in other fields such as agriculture, animal hus-bandry, and economics? All can serve in fields of their specific training, plus serving in sharing the gospel.

One of the most effective pieces of mission work of which I am aware is being done by a former missionary. During his first term as a missionary, where he was in charge of a large publishing house, he had to take an early furlough due to his wife's health. Subsequent develop-ments prevented his continuing in that work. In a conference with me he said, "I cannot return to my appointment, but I have not lost my call from God to be a missionary." He stated his desire to find employment which would place him in countries where we had missionary work. Eventually he was employed by the federal government to work in the AID program in South Vietnam. Five days each week he worked for the government. The other two days were his own. He contacted the missionaries and spent his weekends working with them. Later he repeated the same course in Ethiopia and now in Santo Domingo. He says that he is doing more preaching now than when he was a duly appointed missionary.

These are but examples of what can be done when God's people are willing in the day of his power. They illustrate the fact that the time has come when we need to reexamine our missionary strategy. The old ways are good, but they can be made better by yoking them with new and daring ways to reach the world with the gospel. Many phases of government are beginning to operate under a "sunshine law." Periodically agencies and programs are required to justify their continuance. Such a plan should be followed in spiritual work. No method is sacrosanct simply because it is old. No new proposal should be considered evil or good because it is new. Each should be required to stand on its own merits.

No treatment of this theme would be complete without considering modern means of travel and communication. Whereas the Judsons and Rice spent months going from the United States to their intended mission posts, one can now travel to any part of the globe in a matter of hours. This has already resulted in an adjustment for missionaries in length of service between furloughs as well as the length of the furloughs themselves. These two things serve to make mission service more attractive. It may sound strange to those who stay at home, but a furlough of a year is for most missionaries a burden. It keeps them away from home too long and poses added burdens for those on the mission field while they are away. The little daughter of a missionary couple on furlough from Brazil asked her father, "Daddy, when are we going home?" He said, "Why, honey, we are at home." She replied, "Aw, daddy, this is not home. Brazil is our home!" So it is, and so it should be for effective missionary work.

And then there is the matter of rapid communications. The battle of New Orleans was fought two weeks after the War of 1812 was officially over—so slow were communications then. Now we have instant news with pictures, no less, of events around the globe. We have long spoken of preaching the gospel to the entire human race. Now for the first time in history we have at our disposal the means whereby this can be done. This means is electronics: radio and television.

For eighteen years it was my privilege to be the preacher on "The Baptist Hour," the international radio gospel program of Southern Baptists. It was a labor of love. At a dinner given on the occasion of my retirement from the program, Paul M. Stevens, president of the Southern Baptist Radio and Television Commission, said that for those years weekly I had preached to a potential audience of one hundred million people.

During much of this time through cooperation between the Commission and the Foreign Mission Board, this weekly program in English was broadcast over "The Voice of the Orient" out of Manila and beamed to India. This is the second most populous nation on earth and one in which English is almost a universal language. In addition to local radio stations, the people listen mostly to BBC and "The Voice of the Orient." God alone knows how many people each week heard the gospel in sermon and song. Due to regulations by the Indian government, visas are issued only to missionaries of those religious groups previously established there. That means that Southern Baptists cannot send missionaries to India. But radio waves recognize no boundaries and need no visas. Taped programs are provided to local stations which then give the time as a public service. Just think what could be accomplished if funds were provided for purchasing prime time on ten thousand stations, with the sermons translated into different languages! It should, it could, and it can be done!

Television offers an even greater opportunity. This was clearly demonstrated at the 1977 session of the Southern Baptist Convention. By way of a satellite a live television interview was presented between a spokesman on the platform and a missionary and native pastor in Hong Kong, over six thousand miles away on the opposite side of the earth. The messengers at the Convention viewed it on large screens. At the close of the interview the Hong Kong pastor led everyone in praying together the "Model Prayer." Thus in dramatic fashion was demonstrated the fact that by means of television and the satellite the gospel could be preached to the entire world at one time. It would cost an enormous sum of money, but the impact would be tremendous.

George W. Truett was fond of saying, "Wisdom is fled from us" if we do not do certain things. Surely wisdom is fled from us if we do not rise to the challenge and pay the price in the full dedication of our resources by using every means God has placed in our hands to evangelize the world. "For unto whomsoever much is given, of him shall be much required" (Luke 12:48).

Call to Action

Yes, the future is now! Through the needs of the world God is calling his people to action. Jesus' commission is not to appoint a committee to study the matter. In the Great Commission the imperative verb is not "go" but "teach" or *disciple* (Matt. 28:19–20). "Go" is a participle—"as you go." Not for one moment did Jesus entertain the thought that his people would not go. He simply told them what to do as they went. Those who cannot go should *send* and *support* those who do go. Jesus promised his presence as we do his will. "Lo, I am with you alway" (v. 20). All the days—"even unto the full consummation of the age."

The grandest eras of Christianity have been those when the Lord's people have risen to meet a challenge. There is a worldwide battle being waged for men's bodies, minds, and souls. It is a struggle between tyranny and freedom, atheism and faith, Communism and Christianity. The basic elements in them are very similar up to a point. But Communism gives to them a materialistic rather than a spiritual meaning. It denies every one of the six axioms treated in this book. It certainly denies the competency of the soul in religion.

We cannot defeat Communism by killing Communists. Communism is an idea that can be destroyed only by a better idea. We have that infinitely better idea in the gospel, if only we will use it. If the past fifty years have proved anything in this conflict, it is that governments can neither contain nor destroy Communism through diplomacy or military might. It feeds upon international crises and human misery.

Since men and their plans have failed, we need to give God a chance. And he chooses to work through his people. If we depend only upon human beings, we get only what they can do. If we depend upon God, then we receive what God can do. The old challenge is still true that the world has yet to see what God can do through a man (other than the God-Man, Jesus) who is completely committed to his will. Our generation should show what he can do not through just one man but through multitudes of men and women totally dedicated to do God's will.

The day is far spent. The night is at hand. The King's business calls for haste. And to paraphrase our Lord's words, "We must work the works of him who sent us, while it still is day: the night comes, when no man can work" (cf. John 9:4).